THE FIRST MATILDAS
The 1975 Asian Ladies Championship

THE FIRST MATILDAS
The 1975 Asian Ladies Championship

GREG DOWNES

First published in 2023 by Fair Play Publishing
PO Box 4101, Balgowlah Heights, NSW 2093, Australia
www.fairplaypublishing.com.au

ISBN: 978-1-925914-52-8

ISBN: 978-1-925914-53-5 (ePub)

© Greg Downes 2023

The moral rights of the author have been asserted.
All rights reserved. Except as permitted under the *Australian Copyright Act 1968* (for example, a fair dealing for the purposes of study, research, criticism or review), no part of this book may be reproduced, stored in a retrieval system, communicated or transmitted in any form or by any means without prior written permission from the Publisher.

All images supplied by members of the 1975 team.
Front cover: *Modelling the strip to be worn in the tournament.*
Back cover: *A close-up of the crest on the shirts.*
Cover design and typesetting by Leslie Priestley
Edited by Shannon Mooney

All inquiries should be made to the Publisher via hello@fairplaypublishing.com.au

NATIONAL
LIBRARY
OF AUSTRALIA

A catalogue record of this book is available from the National Library of Australia.

CONTENTS

Foreword by Alen Stajcic	1
Introduction	3
Part 1 – Beginnings to 1968	9
Part 2 – 1968 to 1975	31
Part 3 – The 1975ers	71
Part 4 – 1976 and Beyond	99
Part 5 – Facts, the Fight, and the Future	124
References	132
Acknowledgements	134
About the Author	135

FOREWORD

What a time to be involved in women's football!

Australia is buzzing with anticipation as the July 2023 Women's World Cup approaches to be played in part on home turf. Young women all over Australia and New Zealand are breathless with excitement as they imagine what this could do for their careers, for the nation, and for the game they love, domestically and internationally alike. Between the World Cup, improving player conditions, the success of Australian players in overseas leagues, and the rise of women's sport more generally around the world, women's football in Australia is really getting its time in the spotlight.

As we look ahead, we also look back.

Every player I have coached can tell you of my love of history, football history to be more precise. As a point of a reflection it can be nostalgic. However, the power comes from the learnings and growth we get from lessons learnt and the understanding of what came before us. In my view, for Australian football to sustain consistent growth, we must infuse our football culture with the essence of the struggles of those that came before.

So who were the foremothers of the sport? Who does history have to thank for its current and future success?

The answer to that, of course, is that there are many. Some whose names are well known and who have been prominent and influential in the sport for some time. But there are others who have been in the background, hoping that one day their accomplishment as the first team to represent Australia internationally, would equally be respected and recognised.

In *The First Matildas*, Dr Greg Downes speaks to most of the women involved in the 1975 team who were, indeed, the first team to represent Australia overseas at an international tournament organised by the Asian Football Confederation. While the team was comprised largely of the members of one club, it was also sanctioned by the Australian Soccer Federation, the 1975 equivalent to Football Australia. They wore green and gold. They had the Australian crest on their shirts. They competed as an 'Australia XI' as was the norm. They played under an Australian flag. And they had the obligatory kangaroo as a mascot.

The 1975 tournament was a turning point for women's football in Australia, and it is clear that the women who were part of it are amongst the pioneers who paved the way for the success that women's football enjoys today. Their legacy serves as an inspiration to the current generation of players and the future, too. From Pat O'Connor to Sue Larsen, to Mary Fowler and Gundy's little granddaughter, Matilda, each woman has played a part in passing the global game to the next generation.

It is essential that each successive generation not only remembers and respects what came before them, but most importantly be grateful for the paths that were created from the blood, sweat and tears of others.

Alen Stajcic
Head Coach, Philippines Women's National Team

INTRODUCTION
The 1920s-1950s

Australian women, like their compatriots in the UK and the US, were experiencing unprecedented growth in their freedoms as the 1920s swung into play. Victorian ideals were being swept away, and women were everywhere—in the workplace, in medicine, and even—with the 1925 appointment of Millicent Preston-Stanley to the New South Wales Legislative Assembly—in politics. It's only natural that sport was part of this revolution as well. Sport, especially a game such as football, is as essential to a culture as any song or painting, and nobody knows that more than its players and fans.

One of those players was Alma Kelly, a young woman from the coalfields of the Hunter Valley. She was born in 1910 or 1911 and joined the Weston women's team when she was 17 or 18. Described as a "gregarious, larger-than-life figure," she quickly became a favourite amongst her teammates, even becoming their captain. For the rest of her short life, Alma pushed for the importance of women's football and the right of women to play.

Close to 250 kilometres away, in Sydney, Maisie Alexander spent the latter half of the 1910s playing in England, Canada, and New Zealand before returning to her homeland. Back in Australia, in 1921 she was appointed as head of the Sydney Ladies' Soccer Association.

Both Alma and Maisie probably served as an inspiration for many other young women down the line as the game continued to grow in the country slowly but surely.

Daphne Martin played for the Granville club in western Sydney during the Second World War. She'd gone from munitions to midfield after leaving the factory to help her family in their hamburger shop and needing an outlet for her physical energy. So, at a dance with her friends, Martin formed a team.

And that wasn't the only one! Teams need other teams to play against! In 1942, Granville played a team called Central and caused quite a scandal. After all, they weren't just women. Some of them were *even married!* One, Martha Sheldrick, even parked her toddler's pram on the sidelines before a game.

There are hundreds more stories like this—probably thousands of them. Sadly, those we know now can only be gleaned through old newspaper snippets, long-held family gossip, or closely guarded keepsakes from friends. The vast majority of these stories don't even have these kinds of background and, sadly, the tales of these women pioneers have been lost to history.

But eventually, the slow growth blossomed, and the bright, brilliant petals emerged.

The 1960s and on

The 1960s arrived and brought the Women's Liberation Movement with it. As women strived for freedom across Australia, they found a sense of it on the pitch. Reports from Victoria, New South Wales, and Queensland saw women's teams popping up all over the place, like a current of water that would need more than a cork to stop the flow—but any flow needs direction, and Australian women's football needed someone to guide it from the source.

Those guides were the O'Connor's—Pat and Joe, the godparents of history in the making.

The Controversy

In 1975, a team from Australia took part in a six-nation tournament, the very first Asian Women's Cup run by the Asian Ladies Football Confederation (ALFC). The team was made up of:

- Pat O'Connor – Captain
- Christel Abenthum
- Sue Binns
- Kim Coates
- Julie Dolan AM
- Lynn Everett-Miller

THE FIRST MATILDAS

- Trudy Fischer
- Cindy Heydon
- Vickie Kohen
- Sue Larsen
- Lynn McKenzie
- Connie Selby
- Trixie Tagg
- Sue Taylor
- Aunty Tarita Yvonne Peters (then known as Stacey Tracy)
- Gundy Zarins

These women, many would argue, could be and *should* be recognised as the first Matildas. After all, they competed as a team from Australia sanctioned by the then Australian Soccer Federation, competing against other sanctioned teams from New Zealand, Thailand, Malaysia, Singapore, and Hong Kong. It would be hard to argue that this wasn't a truly international tournament, and that the players in it were not national teams!

These 1975ers, for the most part, expected to finally gain this recognition after a long battle and series of negotiations with Football Australia (FA) over many years. With the upcoming 2023 World Cup and the increase in recognition for women's football, it seemed like the perfect time to acknowledge their place in football history.

But when FA gave a statement in May 2022, it wasn't exactly what the team wanted to hear:

> The women who have been recognised today for their accomplishments are a shining example of the rich history of football in our country, which is so closely linked to the Australian story. We are proud to welcome them into the national team's family.

They "welcomed" the team—a team which has been an essential part of football history for nearly half a century already! After years of fighting for recognition, many members of the team saw this as an insult rather than any movement forward. In fact, a majority of members of the 1975ers decided to reject the peace offering and instead keep fighting for recognition.

So why did these women never receive their numbered caps? FA's official statement on the matter is quite vague. They state that, *"while a historically significant team, the team did not meet the criteria to be categorised as an Australian Senior National Women's Team."*

This was, apparently, a decision recommended by the history committee. But what were the criteria? There is no clear answer. The fact is, though, there can only ever be one criterion when reflecting on history—to borrow a quotation from writer Bonita Mersiades on this subject: *"While history is always relevant, there are other considerations too: fairness, justice, common sense, historical context, gender equity—and the pub test."*

Let's break that down.

Fairness and justice

It is a fact, regardless of whatever politics take place in the background, that the 1975ers played in national colours, sanctioned by the then equivalent of today's FA, in an international tournament against several other countries. Is it just that, all this time later, the importance of that fact is only now truly recognised? And is it fair that, due to vague criteria, they are told that it isn't *enough* to earn them their caps?

Common Sense

Common sense—what's the definition of a national team? "A soccer/football team that represents a particular nation in an international tournament". By applying common sense to the story of the 1975ers, is there any way to say they don't fit into this definition?

Historical context and gender equity

Football hasn't always been what it is now, and that goes triple for women's football. Looking at the historical context of the 1975ers and their achievements, can we shine more of a light on the politics of the situation? In this book, we'll go into more detail about their stories, and in turn glean a more contextual truth.

As pointed out by Mersiades in the article referenced earlier:

The view of the historians is apparently that because "there was not a competitive process to select the team", it is not really an Australian team.

But this ignores one important part of history, and that is historical context.

In 1975, the then nascent Australian Women's Soccer Association was responsible for state and national championships, but they were not involved in international competition and could not be because they were not the official member of FIFA—the ASF was.

And so, if the 1922 team is recognised as the original Socceroos based on the historical context of the time, then how can it be in doubt that the 1975ers were the true First Matildas?

While today's FA point to a lack of written evidence to support the ASF's decision, the fact is, as this book shows, we have the oral testimony of the women involved including those such as Pat O'Connor who have received the highest recognition from FA as pioneers of the game in Australia. Her evidence along should be enough to support the claims of the 1975ers.

Again context is important. Men controlled football in the early 1970s. The women's game was in its infancy and was generally not supported by the male dominated organisations. There is a strong argument that suggests documented (written) history is often in the hands of those in power, and the documentation of the early years of women's football was clearly not of importance to those running the game at that point.

This is supported by the failure to locate any of the relevant written history of the AWSA.

The Pub Test

If we brought up the achievements of the 1975ers in a pub rather than in an FA boardroom, would the results have been different? Just how much headway would the voices of ordinary people have made to the women's fight for recognition as representatives of their country?

An article by Selina Steele quotes renowned journalist and historian Ted Simmons with a suggestion on the issue—not to renumber all the caps, but to

THE FIRST MATILDAS

give these women their acknowledgement and assign them Roman numerals on their caps. It would not only be fair, but an answer that everyone in the pub would surely get behind.

The Stories

Everyone has a story. Starting from the very beginning, the stories told in these pages take in the point of view of women who up until now have been silent, and puts it all in the context they truly deserve—often in their own words.

They are the 1975ers. The first Australian national side.

The First Matildas.

Part 1
BEGINNINGS TO 1968
Pat and Joe O'Connor

I'm getting on a bit now. Maybe not so much for me, but for the rest of the girls, they really played their hearts out, and I think that some kind of recognition would be fantastic.

Teammate Trixie Tagg referred to Pat and Joe O'Connor as "the godfather and godmother of women's football in Australia," and it is, by far, a fitting description. The O'Connors were British immigrants who came to the game in the 1960s; football provided an opportunity for them both to become involved in the local sporting culture. It was an important decade, especially in the historical context, as it became the decade now widely recognised as the period in which the women's game became firmly established in Australia.

Over their 15 years of involvement, between 1963 and 1978, the couple were instrumental in developing and formalising many aspects of the modern game, including the creation of the Metropolitan Ladies Soccer Association (MLSA), NSW Ladies Soccer Federation, and the Australian Women's Soccer Association (AWSA). They also played a major role in the presentation of the women's game in the international arena, with the Asian Ladies Soccer Confederation (ALSC). Most importantly for this book, they were the driving force behind the first national women's team to represent Australia at an international tournament—at the 1975 Asian Women's Cup.

Joe O'Connor was born in 1933 in a small town called Cahir, located in the County of Tipperary, Ireland, as one of eleven children. Due to the economic conditions in Ireland in the 1950s, Joe emigrated to England at the age of 21, where he worked in various small jobs before taking up a position building electric transmission towers. The work took him all over England.

Pat was born in 1941 in Nuneaton, northern Warwickshire, England. As it happened, Joe's sister met and married Pat's brother and through this, Joe and Pat met at a young age. In her own words, Pat describes her family as:

> A typical Irish family. Joe's sister married my brother. Although Joe was eight years older than me, I've known him for a long time—since I was a kid. He worked on building the electric pylons (transmission towers) in England. So, he travelled all over the place. He used to come back to see his sister every now and again.
>
> When he first came over, he was doing various small jobs. And then he met someone, and they said, "Come and join us!" He did, and travelled all over the place. We got together. I was very young. We got married and we travelled all over England with the job until we came to Australia. So, we saw most of England as well.

In 1963, the pair made the decision together to move to Australia. Pat explains the reasons behind this choice:

> We always wanted to come to Australia, mainly because of the weather, I must admit. The English weather for people who like the outdoors is not great. Joe was a bodybuilder and weightlifter when he was in England. That was his hobby. He won various competitions bodybuilding and got a couple of medals for weightlifting. He was a real outdoors type.

Even though he was a weightlifter and an outdoorsman, and Pat liked the outdoors too, football wasn't really on their horizon. While Joe had played some football in Ireland (as a goalkeeper for the local Cahir Town Football Club), Pat had no interest in the game at all. Due to the traveling required by Joe's employment, joining a football club was difficult and his interest in bodybuilding and weightlifting led him to joining gyms all over the country as he travelled. Now, though, in Australia, things would change.

We came to Australia in 1963 and we spent six months in the Villawood Hostel. And then we saved everything we could to buy a house—not far away from the hostel actually—just to get into the housing market. It was right opposite the Bass Hill RSL Club, and our son, Kirk, was in Year 6 at the time and was going to the local Catholic School.

Of all things, a note from Kirk's school would be the unexpected spark that ignited the flame. A simple leaflet would turn the O'Connors into legends, and lead to the rapid development of women's football—not only in NSW, but also across the nation.

Kirk was sent home with a note asking if he'd like to join the Bass Hill RSL Soccer Club as an Under 7. His parents thought it was a great idea and took him along and signed him up. While they were there, Pat and Joe noticed that several of the women—the mums, sisters, and daughters—were also playing a game, the Bass Hill mums and sisters against the visitors. The O'Connors stopped to watch, and at Joe's encouragement, Pat decided to go and ask to join in.

I'd never kicked a ball before. I didn't know anything about kicking a soccer ball, and I'd never really been an actual soccer fan, although my brother played local soccer back home and my dad was a referee. But I'd never really had anything to do with it.

I went over to the coach and said I was interested, and he said, "OK, we're going to have a run next Tuesday just to get the girls together before the beginning of the season. Come over and have a kick around."

So I went. He said, "Which foot do you kick with?' and I said "left". He just threw me the number 10 shirt and said, "I need somebody to score goals. That's your job", and that was it. I didn't know what to do!

Well, I mean, I was in my 20s when I joined Bass Hill RSL Ladies' team. I didn't have anything at all to do with soccer up until then. Not even in England.

My father was a local referee in England and my brother played for my local town team. But I didn't kick a ball or anything. I had nothing whatsoever to do with soccer until 1965. But I do remember being very proud and sending newspaper clippings and some photos back to my dad in England. He sent them to our local newspaper in Nuneaton, and there was a big splash in the local newspaper, and he was so proud.

You know I was playing soccer and carrying on the family tradition, I guess.

When Pat joined Bass Hill, it was a social team. They were just groups of women who got together to play other women who travelled around following their sons' games—soon, however, all that would change.

Apart from his earlier stint in goal for Cahir Town, Joe had little more to do with the game up until his son and wife got involved. But, after a while, attending all of Pat's matches, Joe was asked if he wanted to become the assistant coach of the team, to which he agreed. After a year, when the man running the team decided to move on, Joe took over as the head coach.

The women at Bass Hill RSL played social games against other locally formed teams from Blacktown, Bankstown, and Sydney. However, after spending one year with Bass Hill, the women decided that they would like to take the game more seriously. Pat became captain and Joe coach during the 1966 season, and then they made their move.

At the end of the season, Joe and I put an ad in a Sydney newspaper for those interested in forming a team. This was going to be serious soccer. We wanted to play proper soccer, and anyone who was interested I gave them my phone number. Gee, I got quite a few responses, and all of a sudden, we had a team!

And so, what would in a few years become the basis of the legendary 1975ers began to come together.

We had one or two girls that were the basis of the team that had played before. Trixie Tagg had kicked a ball in Holland with the guys and Christel Abenthum had played in Germany. Two girls, Pat Redmond and her friend Margaret, were attached to the Manchester City team in England, and we had a few girls that knew what it was all about. And a girl called Ann Hamilton who played in Scotland. We also got a few lovely local girls joining in.

THE FIRST MATILDAS

A weekly national newspaper, *Soccer World* (also known as the *Green Paper*), established by Hungarian immigrants in 1953, provided a source for new Australians to learn about the game in Australia. It acted as a main point of promotion. The paper promised to act as a link between Australians and new Australians in bringing them together on the field of sport.

There is a historical narrative here: that there was little attention paid to the women's game by the media, or that everything that was written was disdainful, but that isn't entirely true—at least, not in Pat's experience. The O'Connors were regular contributors to the Green Paper, and appeared in several other noted media sources.

> Joe and I made sure of that, we contacted everybody, and we were on first name terms with the guys in the *Green Paper*. We were actually putting articles in the papers, and we were even having people asking us for stories. But gosh, they were contacting us all the time for news because it was new. They wanted to know about it, everyone associated with soccer.
>
> There was a magazine called *Pix People*. And we had double page spread in that and in *The Telegraph*. Because the only way we could let people know we were there was to keep putting articles in the paper. We had our results published, loads and loads of stories about different things that happened. And that's how we got a lot of contacts with people.
>
> I had no negatives from anyone in the newspapers or the soccer clubs or anywhere.

Pat's great experience with the media was essential to her success. Many journalists were, indeed, an important part of supporting women's sport in the 60s and 70s, the era where it was starting to take off. As teammate Kay De Bry succinctly explained, *"If you don't get media coverage, you don't get sponsorship and you don't get anything."*

Recognition, in other words, was everything, even then. Fortunately, at least in the media sense, Pat and Joe were able to secure that for their team.

In fact, it was a newspaper article that caught the attention of not only women keen to get involved—but football officials who would help the O'Connors change the face of the women's game forever. Pat explains,

> I received a phone call from one of the officials at the Prague men's team who were in the National League competition at the time. He was a committee member, and he said, 'I saw your ad in the paper and when you get your team together, would you like to come over and be the Prague women's team?' Actually, his daughter and her friend were keen to play so that was an incentive for him. I think they were quite young, only 15 or so. We thought this is good, this is brilliant. So, we did.

It was the perfect spot in history for Pat's team to strike. During the 1960s and 1970s, women were gradually able to subvert those embedded male attitudes of discrimination and marginalisation on and off the field. Women's teams were formed in increasing numbers, some inside clubs and many independently. Sympathetic male coaches, referees, and administrators were recruited to support the establishment of women's leagues and associations, though the bulk of the driving was still done by the women themselves.

In complete contrast to the experiences of other women trying to gain access to the male-dominated and controlled game in other parts of Australia at this time, the women had been openly invited to become part of one of Sydney's prominent men's soccer clubs. And so, the O'Connors agreed to the meeting.

> Joe and I had a meeting with the Prague committee, and look, I have to say this from the start—every relationship we had with any form of the men's game from the word go, they were extremely supportive. We never had anyone that said, you know, "you're only a bunch of girls" or anything like that, anything derogatory. From the word go, we were given every opportunity to play good soccer.
>
> The Prague club started us off with some uniforms; they organised training grounds, and they allowed us, after a while, to play some exhibition matches in the half time period of the men's games.

In 1967, the team went over to Prague. During this period, the women's team had an exhibition match played prior to a men's Australian Cup match at E.S Marks field on 31st March 1967. Prague ladies played GM United Ladies. The men's game was between St George and South Sydney Croatia, as Sydney United were known in those days.

And so, with the support of their new team behind them, Pat and Joe began the next chapter.

Trixie Tagg

I can now stand up tall when people remind me that the journey had to start somewhere and our team, our groups or clubs were part of the journey. And now to see the Women's World Cup 2023. Oh, my goodness. I'm so excited.

Trixie has a place of honour in Australian women's football history. She is significant as a player-administrator and for being the first female Matildas coach, but some of her proudest and fondest memories go back to playing on that 1975 team. Even after that, Trixie was appointed the National Coach in 1981 for the tour to New Zealand. Eight Matildas earned their first commemorative Cap during this tour. She also held a number of administrative positions in the AWSA, from 1977 to 1981.

Like Pat and Joe, Trixie was part of the influx of post-war immigrants to Australia that lasted through to the 1960s. She migrated in 1962 from the Netherlands and quickly got involved in the Australian women's football scene.

Trixie was born Trixie van Lieshout in Amsterdam, the Netherlands, in 1948. She was one of six children. As there was no organised football for boys until the age of 12, and nothing at all for girls, Trixie came to the game at the age of eight by joining a local street gang and playing whenever she got the opportunity. She describes how football was a part of her life from a young age in her own words:

> In Amsterdam, I was part of a lovely street gang. They were boys and they accepted me as an equal. Every opportunity I had, we played football in the schools, and there was a neighbourhood centre that opened up for many hours on weekends. We always played there as well. They accepted me as an equal and that's where I learned a lot of my basic skills and love of the game.

When Trixie, three of her siblings, and her parents arrived in Australia in 1962, they set up home in the southern suburbs of Sydney. Like Pat and Joe, Trixie's family initially stayed in the migrant hostels in Villawood, and eventually moved to a rented house in Carlton for a few years. Then, when her parents had finally saved enough money, they moved into a house of their own—a little cottage in St. Georges Parade, Hurstville.

Although women were playing football in Australia in the early 1960s, it was mostly social and unstructured. Trixie loved sports and loved competitive play, but since that wasn't an option for girls at the time, she took another route.

> But when we emigrated to Australia for five years there was nothing, so I ended up playing hockey at Kogarah High School. I thought that hockey was a little bit similar to soccer with a team formation and defined skills. It sort of gave me a lifeline.

But Trixie always yearned for the game she loved. In 1967, Trixie noticed Pat O'Connor's advertisement in the *Sydney Telegraph*, a local newspaper—the call to interested women who were keen to play soccer led her to Pat and Joe O'Connor, and the start of a lifelong friendship. It also became the launch of her football journey in Australia, one that would last a lifetime.

> When I saw Pat O'Connor's little article in the newspaper, my goodness, well, all my birthdays came at once.
> That was the first time ever that I saw that girls could play soccer. I hadn't seen any girls' soccer since I arrived in 1962. I had been devastated, but this opened the door for me. I quickly phoned Pat from work. She said, "Come to training Thursday night at E.S Marks Field", and I did. And on that Sunday 31st of March, a few days later I played my first game.

And what a game it was—the curtain-opener game that showed people just how serious and intriguing women's football could be. Trixie stayed with the team for a long time after that. After all, football had always been in her blood.

Christel Abenthum

I'm proud to be part of the beginning.

Like Trixie, Christel Abenthum began playing football on the streets of Berlin with the boys from the local neighbourhood. Christel came by ship to Australia in 1966 and began her football career in Sydney at the age of 22 with Prague Ladies FC in 1968. She was good enough to be selected to play professionally for Bayern Munich on a return trip to Europe in 1974 and was one of the first women players to represent Australia at the inaugural Asian Women's Cup in Hong Kong in 1975. Christel was a striker and played up front alongside Pat O'Connor.

Christel was born in 1945 in Berlin. She has three siblings, two sisters and a younger brother. Christel came to Australia on the Honda Lena Lauro with her brother, arriving in March 1966 at the age of 21.

> As a migrant I signed up for two years because my brother, he wanted to come—he's a waiter by trade—but he was underage—you had to be 21. And I said, "Well, I'll come with you." I had just turned 21.

Life as an emigrant in 1960s Australia was not an easy one, especially for those who couldn't speak English well and had to wrestle with cultural prejudices that made it difficult for women to find work in male-dominated professions. Many professionally trained women had to settle for menial work in order to survive.

Christel's brother was able to find a job as a waiter but, even though she was a mechanic by trade, she had a much more difficult time. Whenever she made queries, she was told that *"women don't work on cars"*, and so she struggled to find a job at all.

> I looked around and, I mean, I couldn't speak English so, I worked in a kitchen, washing dishes and then cleaning the rooms in a Kings Cross motel. I was working there, and they said that once my English improved, I could serve breakfast.
>
> One fella we met once said, "Oh, you're German". So, we started talking and he was working as a mechanic at a service station and said, "Why don't you come and work and show them what you can do?"
>
> So I worked and yeah, everything was good, but then they didn't have separate toilets. He said, "I'm sorry but I can't employ you because they need to be separate."

Eventually she found a position at a service station in Darlinghurst, Sydney, looking after one of three stations operating in the area. Christel lived in Kings Cross, renting a room for $10 a week on a wage of only $30.

When I went to work, I went to the bus stop and he said, take a bus because it's quite a long way to go to the motel to work, and the bus never stopped, so I had to walk. I was late the first day, because I didn't know that you have to put your hand out to stop the bus. Nobody told me!

Christel's involvement in football in Germany was restricted to playing with the boys in the street, as there was no other option for girls to play the game. The German Football Association (DFB) had banned women from playing the game in 1955 due to the alleged health consequences and the associated reputation attached to women playing the game. Many still believed that playing the game had a negative impact on the women's ability to give birth, on their soul, and female grace. This wouldn't change until 1970, long after Christel had left for Australia.

Football clubs and the football establishment in the 1960s were male-run, and as such, discrimination against women playing football was widespread. Women looking to play football were not generally supported by the male-dominated clubs, particularly in Europe during this time. This is evident in the reply Christel received from the Hanover Football Club when she queried them. She still has the original letter all these years later.

And then there was the time a team started up somewhere in Germany—in Hanover. I sent them a letter, I said "Oh look, I've just come from Berlin to Hanover. I just want to play the game and I've still got the letter today." He said:
"Look, just get married and then you go with your husband to the soccer field, watch the soccer and then you go home and cook".
That was a full stop for soccer, but that's when I came to Australia.

One year after arriving in Australia, Christel read about women playing football—she noticed the advertisement that Pat and Joe O'Connor had placed in *The Sydney Telegraph*. Christel was then living in Lane Cove with her parents who had travelled to Australia to be with their children. And that's how her football journey began.

Gundy Zarins

Anyone who represents his or her country, I think, deserves recognition.

Gundy didn't meet Pat and Joe O'Connor or become involved in the team that would become the 1975ers until 1971. However, even before that, football was an important part of her life.

Gundy was born in Stanmore, Sydney, in 1953, but spent her early childhood in Engadine, a southern suburb of the city. Gundy's parents fled from Latvia to Germany as refugees at the end of WWII to escape the impending arrival of the Soviet occupational forces that entered the country towards the end of the war, before ultimately ending up in Australia.

> My parents left Latvia in 1944 with my sister who was two at the time, and went to Germany as refugees. They stayed there for about five years. My brother was born in Germany in 1948. They all came to Australia in 1949. And I was born in 1953.
>
> Latvia is a sporting nation, everyone plays sport. Doesn't matter if you're an intellectual or artist, labourer, academic or office worker. Everyone plays some sort of ball sport. Latvia won the first European Basketball Championships in 1935.
>
> My mom was an intellectual, she didn't like sport at all. Dad was the biggest supporter. He was a javelin thrower. He followed Arsenal in the English Premier League and St. George here. He enjoyed all sports.

By 1968, 15-year-old Gundy had little way to access the women's game in the climate of Australia at the time. Seven years from then, however, she'd become part of the first national team.

Julie Dolan AM

That's why these women and the people like Joe were so instrumental in getting the game a much higher profile, even though the profile wasn't that high in those days.

Without that push, without that relentless campaigning, we wouldn't have gotten to where we did.

Julie Dolan is one of the most highly respected pioneers of the women's game in Australia. From fighting over a football with her brothers in a backyard in Sydney as a child, Julie went on to captain Australia at the age of 18 and become the recipient of the number one commemorative cap in recognition as a Matilda in 1979.

Julie played a total of 34 matches for the Matildas, including 18 capped Internationals. In 1996-97 the Julie Dolan medal was created for best player in the Women's National Soccer League, and later the W League each year, and in 1999 she was enrolled in the FFA Hall of Fame. Her involvement continued for decades; in 2016, FFA added her name to their annual celebration of achievements. These are the Dolan Warren Awards that highlight the best female and male player, voted by the players. Julie was awarded an OAM in 2018 in recognition of her services to football.

Julie Dolan was only 14 when she toured as a member of the first Australian eleven at the inaugural Asian Women's Cup in Hong Kong in 1975. Julie played in the midfield and was selected in the first game against Thailand. She is now recognised as one of the best Australia has produced in that position.

Because of her age, she didn't get involved with the team or with Pat and Joe until 1975. In 1968, she hadn't even started playing football, but when she did, it set the course of her life.

Julie was born in Sydney in 1961. She began playing football in her backyard with her four brothers at the age of eight.

> [I played] informally in the backyard with my four brothers. And as most people did back then, we played in the backyard, all sorts of games, and footy seemed to be an easy one for everyone to get involved with. So that's where I had my inauspicious start, fighting with the boys in the backyard.

As a young girl, she was able to play in a boys' team, since there were no girls' teams available, but she showed remarkable talent.

I was interested in playing, and especially playing in a women's team, but there wasn't that much around at the time. But initially I played in the boys' team at Heathcoat High School when they would allow me to play. I played quite a few competition games against other schools there. But after that there wasn't much going around. Nothing that we knew of that was formally organised.

Julie was eager to play competitively though and, unknowingly, she followed in the footsteps of her future teammate, Trixie. Until she came across her future team in 1971, Julie was heavily involved in women's hockey, even playing at a state level.

Kay De Bry (née Kress)

In all honesty we were the first Australian team to go and play in an international tournament.

Kay didn't meet Pat and Joe or even become involved in football until 1974, but she has always been involved in sport. In fact, she was President of the Women in Sport Foundation in 1974 when she met Pat and Joe O'Connor at a women's soccer match at Wentworth Park in Sydney. This meeting launched Kay's role as a pioneer in the development of women's soccer in the Eastern Suburbs of Sydney and as a key organiser of the first Australian eleven.

She was born in Hobart in 1948. Kay became involved in soccer while President of the Women in Sport Foundation and a keen netballer in 1974. Kay did not play in the 1975 team, but she was still an important part of it.

Sue Binns

I love soccer and I was happy I was chosen.

Sue Binns grew up in the Western suburbs of Sydney as the only girl in a family of three brothers. Sue's love of sport led her to football in the early 1970s and her skill and determination caught the attention of the then coach of the Ingleburn RSL women's team, Jim Selby. She was handpicked to tour internationally when the team travelled to New Zealand in early 1975 to play in the Air New Zealand

Cup series. As a result of the team's success and Sue's contribution, Jim Selby recommended Sue to Joe O'Connor who was the coach of the mighty St George Budapest team. Sue then found herself on the plane to Hong Kong later that same year as part of an Australian eleven to participate in the inaugural Asian Women's Cup.

Sue was born in Canley Vale, Sydney in 1957. Her family home was located in Guildford, where she began her soccer career in 1970.

Sue is still living in the Western suburbs of Sydney at St Clare.

Kim Coates

Although I know some people don't recognise the 1975 tour as an Australian team, I do. I had the green and gold on and I was never prouder to play for my country than I was in that tournament.

Kim Coates played fullback and represented both NSW and Victoria several times during the 1970s. She began her football career in Blacktown, Sydney and went on to represent her country in 13 appearances between 1978 and 1983. Kim proudly wears the number 5 commemorative cap in recognition of her participation in the first Australian team to be officially recognised by Football Federation Australia (FFA) in the tournament against New Zealand in 1979. Kim also travelled to Hong Kong in 1975 and is an advocate for the recognition of those players who represented their country at that tournament.

She was born in Ryde Hospital, Sydney in 1957. She is one of four children and now resides in Colebee, a suburb in the western region of Sydney. She was introduced to football by her father in 1970.

Lyn Everett-Millar

I just feel I was very fortunate to be part of it.

Lyn Everett-Miller was bought up in a multi-generational family in the 1950s and 1960s in Sydney. Soccer was not a sport that was spoken about let alone played, but a chance meeting with soon-to-be teammate Trixie Tagg, and the influence of Pat and Joe O'Connor led to a lifelong love of football. Lyn played until the age of 58 and was an integral part of the 1975ers team.

Lyn was born in Arncliffe, Sydney, in December 1952, but grew up in Sans Souci with her mum. Her early influences were restricted to the family's involvement with rugby league.

> My parents separated when I was really little. We lived with my grandparents and actually some of my cousins at one stage, but we were a family that was more with rugby league—soccer was something quite foreign to us. The other members of the family or extended family were all rugby league focused, particularly my grandfather because he was a Newtown supporter. And I just remember listening to the games, you know, early days on the radio.
>
> But yeah, soccer wasn't something that we even really knew about it, I don't think.

The role of women in society in Sydney during the 1960s was still restricted by conservative social values, which had persisted since before WWII, and emphasised the importance of family and the primary domestic responsibilities of women. Although by the mid-1960s challenges to this status quo became more prevalent, leading to the rise of the women's movement in the 1970s, it was still a strange time.

> This is the late 60s early 70s and women, as far as I'm concerned, were still pretty much regarded as not being good at a lot of things. When I left school, the High School Certificate had only been in a couple of years, and it wasn't something that a lot of people did, unless you were going to do medicine or something like that. But generally, in those times [a woman] became a teacher, a hairdresser, a nurse or secretary. And that was pretty much it.
>
> I don't think a lot of people thought outside of the box. Well, I know I didn't. But then I might have been the only one. But you know, my parents didn't have a high education, and I don't think it was expected that I would go on to anything else other than finishing Year 10 and getting a job.
>
> I remember going for a loan for a car and they said to me "You probably won't get the loan—you're a female and you, you know you could get

pregnant. And what are we going to do then? How can you repay the loan?" I eventually did get the loan, but it was a strange, strange time.

Lyn left school early at the age of 16 in 1968 but decided to go back and study for her High School Certificate a few years later. It was here that she met Trixie Tagg and that was the beginning of her soccer career.

Aunty Tarita Yvonne Peters (née Stacey Tracy)

I definitely am. I already know that. I am the first Aboriginal lady to play for Australia.

Aunty Tarita Yvonne Peters is an Aboriginal Elder, mentor and role model for promoting interest in women's soccer for Indigenous communities. Her history in the development of women's soccer in Sydney during the 1960s and 70s with the St George Budapest club and touring team has created a lasting legacy. Aunty Tarita was the first Aboriginal woman to play soccer for Australia, and by telling her story she hopes to strengthen the multicultural aspects of the game.

Formerly known as Stacey Tracy, Aunty Tarita was born in 1944 in Urangan, a suburb of Hervey Bay in Queensland. She is proud of her Aboriginal heritage and has changed her name to fully reflect the importance of family in her life.

> I was known as Stacey Tracy then, but I want to get back to being me, so I go under Aunty because I am an elder and I'm Tarita Yvonne. And I'm going to take my family name, Peters, because, my grandfather is from the Keppel islands, and his name is Albert Ross Peters.
>
> My mother is a Wambaya woman. She came from the Northern Territory, just across the border from Mt Isa. A place called Carmerwheel, and she was born at Brunette Station. She was part of the stolen generation at five years old. On my father's side his mother is a Cloncurry Aboriginal woman, and my grandfather is Woppaburra from the Keppel islands. So, I'm surrounded by my heritage.

THE FIRST MATILDAS

My father and grandfather worked, and my mother and my grandmother lived on Fraser Island. They were timber cutters. Dad started working over there when he was ten years old.

My great grandmother was well respected and there's a long story there. She ended up in the Hall of Fame at Longreach. And I've since been told that she's now buried on the Tiwi Islands, so I want to go up there and find out the story on my mother's side of the family.

[The Authorities] took their last names from them and she had such a complicated Aboriginal name that they called her Larry. She was a horse breaker and my Grandmother Amelia, mum's mother, was a horse breaker and my mother could even break horses. So, it's no wonder I liked that exciting side of life.

But as for breaking horses, no, I didn't, but I used to ride those motorbikes well!

Aunty Tarita left Hervey Bay when she was teenager. She headed for Yeppoon, where she met her husband. They decided to move to Sydney together.

I moved from Harvey Bay when I was 17½ years old. I went to a place outside of Yeppoon where my sister was living. Her husband did the tracks on the railway lines. And that's where I met my husband. His family had a service station, and we went up to Rockhampton. He was an apprentice mechanic at the time with Lawrence Motors in Rockhampton.

We were always talking about getting to the Big Smoke. We used to call Sydney the Big Smoke. He had a Triumph motorbike. We put a port on the back with a few clothes and he filled up the saddlebags with his toolkit and we went from Rockhampton all the way to Sydney.

As soon as we arrived, I got the best job in the world. I was working in a lolly factory. I could eat as much as I liked! He worked for International Harvesters. We then moved to Maroubra, to his grandmother's home, and that's where we started off. From there over to Regents Park and from Regents Park, because I had my first child, to East Hills.

From there we rented a farm at Milperra, and I had my second child. So I had the two children and my husband was working at Hawker De Havillands. From there we went into our house in Greenacre.

It was 1967, and Aunty Tarita was 23 years of age when they moved to Greenacre, a western suburb of Sydney. She was working full time as a private investigator, which didn't leave much time for socialising or exercise. Little did she know that the beginning of her time in women's soccer was waiting for her just over the back fence.

I was living in Greenacre in Sydney, and my office and everything was in Bankstown. And one afternoon I'm thinking, "look, I'm working, working, working all the time, I'd like to do something", and I just happened to walk out my back door, and over my fence there is a park, Greenacre Park. There are girls out there kicking a ball, carrying on, and I thought. "I wonder if they would allow me to come and exercise for half an hour with them." And that's the first time I ever saw soccer with the Greenacre girls.

So I jumped the fence and I went over and I said, "Would you mind, I just live over there, and I'd like to get about half an hour's exercise. Can I exercise with you?" And they said, "For sure! Come and join us."

That was at the start of the week, and at the end of the week I played against a team called Prague. I had no idea of the game, but I'm a fast mover and I actually manned the whole area from the back to the front, not really knowing the rules or anything.

And the Prague team, which was the team that went over and became St George, were quite impressed with me. Because I could move and this was my first week. I was only in for half an hour of exercise because I'm a really busy person.

One person from the other side said, "You're really good. If you want to go to a better team, you're very welcome to come and join us." I can't say who said it or whatever because I don't recall, but I was invited.

So, I had another game with Greenacre, and I realised that I seemed to be the only person really doing the job. And so, I don't know how I went about it, but I did join them. I joined Prague and that's how I first got into it. When we played our matches, they started to teach me the better way, but the one thing I had to my advantage was I was always very fast. And no one could ever get past me.

That's about 47 years ago.

That chance encounter would change Aunty Tarita's life, and the life of women's football in Australia forever.

Sue Larsen

It was wonderful, a big part of my life, and I tell people I played for Australia because I believe that I did, and I am proud to hold that honour.

Sue Larsen owes her beginning in football to the dedication and support of her father. She played football for 15 years, starting at the age of ten and finally hanging up her boots at the age of 25. During her career, Sue played with the highly successful Prague Ladies, St George Budapest, and Marconi women's teams. She represented her State of NSW at several national championships throughout the 1970s. Sue also played on the right wing in Hong Kong.

Born in southern suburbs of Sydney in July 1959, Sue started playing football at the age of ten. She is now 62 and living in Queensland but spent all of her football years in NSW. Sue owes her start in football to her late father. He was driving home one day after work and noticed some women playing soccer. Knowing that his daughter was "mad keen" on playing, he pulled over and happened to meet both Pat and Joe O'Connor.

> I started playing when I was 10. My dad was a soccer referee and my brother had played in the past, so I was always mad keen on playing soccer. I used to go to training with my brother and watch my dad referee. He was driving home from work one day and saw some ladies playing soccer. He pulled up and it happened to be Pat and Joe O'Connor. So, he had a chat with Joe and he said, "Bring your daughter along next weekend to this venue."
>
> And that's basically where I started. I went along, they had a training day and that's where I started.

Sue's parents were the main influences in her football career, and in particular the love her dad had of the women's game and the passion he brought to the support he shared.

My mum and dad were extremely supportive of anything that I did, but as I said it was soccer, I loved my soccer. I was pretty good at school, and I was dux at my school one year. I went to Lilly Pilly Primary and then to Caringbah High.

My dad was my rock when it came to soccer. As I said he was always a referee. He was a shift worker, but he would always try and make sure that he was available on a Sunday, whatever shift he could get because he'd come out and referee for us.

You know it got to the stage where other guys would come along and referee as well. Or Dad would always put his hand up saying, "You know, mate, I'll run the line for you," or do something, but I mean he used to come along until I could drive. He used to drive me everywhere and, if he couldn't, my mum used to drive me. He'd take me to training and even when I did start to drive if he could he would still come and he'd run around with us, and you know, kick the ball with us and get involved.

When we'd have team picnics he was always there and he loved the game. He absolutely loved the women's soccer. He said he loved refereeing the ladies better than the men.

He was a huge influence in my life, unfortunately not with me anymore, but he got me right into it and got me started.

My Mum was also involved. She was our manageress for a few years and she and Mrs Kohen (Vickie's mum) would have oranges for half time, cut sandwiches, drinks etc. after the game for everyone. She travelled interstate with me on state championships and was a huge supporter.

Sue was a child when she started out, and she spent her whole football career with Pat and Joe O'Connor, concentrating solely on her game even as she got older, right up until she retired at 25.

I didn't get involved with the administration or the politics or anything like that. I'd go to training, and I was asked to play and basically that's what I did.

THE FIRST MATILDAS

Vickie Dean (née Kohen)

They were probably the best days of my life.

Vickie started her soccer career with the star-studded St George Budapest team in 1970 under the tutelage of Pat and Joe O'Connor. Vickie went on to play for her home state and attributes her 1975 Australian jacket to meeting her husband while at university in the 1980s.

She was born in Canterbury Hospital in Sydney in 1956, the eldest of two, and grew up in Padstow in the Bankstown area. Vickie now lives in Mona Vale on the northern beaches in Sydney. Her involvement in soccer can be traced back to the influence of her younger brother.

> I have a younger brother, Kim, who was quite involved in soccer. He was the reason I started playing. He was quite a good soccer player, so he used to train at the park down the road and I was into all kinds of sport. So, I used to go down and try and talk my way into training with the boys.
>
> Even though they were a couple of years younger than me, they didn't really appreciate having a girl around, I don't think.
>
> We used to constantly play in the back and front yard and kick balls against the walls and knock the fence over because we kicked the balls too hard.
>
> I was reasonably capable. I quite liked it and I very occasionally got to play a social game when my brother was playing in his team if they were short, but other than that I didn't play soccer at all. I had no idea that girls could play and at that stage we weren't supposed to be playing in the boy's team, and when I tried to play on the boy's team, I had to look like a boy!
>
> I probably, in the whole time, only played like two social games with the boys. I wasn't allowed to play in any of their competition games because I was a girl clearly. None of them seemed to know anything about women's soccer either, because if they had I would have been there like a flash. It was just completely unheard of at that stage.

Vickie had the full support of her family, which allowed her to participate not only in soccer—but in any sport that she wanted to play. However, society at the time wasn't quite as accepting.

> I was probably pretty lucky. My parents were really supportive of everything that I did, and I was involved in all sorts of sports. I was a bit unusual anyway as a girl. I did other sports that were unusual, like I used to do judo as well, and I swam. I didn't really get any negatives.
>
> I was involved in the Salvation Army and the church didn't like you playing sport on Sunday, so I used to get some flak for that!
>
> Apart from being called a tomboy, which I was, it was perfectly fine. I do think that women's soccer was still seen as a novelty right up until I stopped playing, I guess.
>
> I remember having to change shirts on the sideline because there were no women's changerooms and how messy and smelly the changerooms were if we got to use the men's ones. I got good at maintaining some degree of modesty when changing shirts!

It wouldn't be until 1970 when Vickie, like so many others, had a chance encounter with Pat and Joe O'Connor that would change her life.

Part 2
1968 TO 1975
Pat and Joe

In 1968, both Pat and Joe undertook a FIFA-endorsed national coaching certificate, which was presented by the Bankstown Soccer Coaching Academy. It was the only official coaching qualification that Joe received throughout his coaching career. However, the Academy took pride in announcing that Mrs Pat O'Connor from the Bass Hill RSL Ladies' team was to be the first lady in Australia to receive such a certificate.

The same year, news of other teams forming began to filter through, so Pat and Joe decided to contact clubs that might have had a women's team and invite them to a meeting. The Metropolitan Ladies Soccer Association was formed in the meeting rooms of the Bankstown United Soccer Clubs Ltd at the start of the 1968 season.

Pat had an idea.

We said, "Let's start a league". They said, "You're mad! We've only got four teams." Joe said, "Well, you've got to start somewhere".

So, in 1968 we formed the Metropolitan Ladies Soccer Association (MLSA), and in that first competition season we had the Prague team, two teams from Riverstone (Riverstone A and B), and then a team from Greenacre Soccer club.

It was open house, not only to our own team but to any girls in any teams in the Metropolitan Association. We had a huge garden, and we had the football field behind the house. We had such a big garden that we put a goal up right at the back and we had shooting practice. Then we put a net up and played foot tennis, and then we put a pool in so we could swim afterwards.

And I tell you one lot would arrive and we'd have a kick with them and as they were leaving another lot would arrive and we'd have a kick with them and that was our life.

The door was open to anybody that wanted to come over and get a bit of exercise. Yeah, it was magic.

Of course, like in any situation, there were politics to consider.

Once we got our soccer going in Sydney, it fell under the banner of the New South Wales Association. We always had our own competition going, but the New South Wales Federation was the governing body. We were just at the Sydney Association when we formed the Federation for women.

After the formation of the first competition, the MLSA organised a number of knockout competitions due to the growing popularity, including the Bankstown Thistles, Hume United, and the Bankstown United Soccer Clubs Ltd Knockout competitions.

During that first season, Prague Ladies played a total of 25 games—winning them all—scoring 180 goals for and only two goals against. In 1969, more teams joined, and the women's game was beginning to grow in the other states as well. Word reached Sydney that a number of teams were forming in Queensland and so the Prague team invited them down to play.

The Annersley Women's team visited to play a friendly match in 1970, which Prague won four goals to two. In fact, the Prague women's team won all three titles between 1967 and 1970, the first against Greenacre Ladies.

After a chat about football with a committee member of a rival club in 1971, Pat and Joe received an offer which heralded the beginning of a period in women's football history that is still unsurpassed today.

I worked with a guy that was on the St George Budapest Soccer Club committee. And he said, "we were just talking about football, do you fancy a change? Come over to St George and see what we can offer you."

So, in 1971, we went over from Prague to St George. No bad blood.

Prague looked after us very well, gave us uniforms, fields to play on. They gave us a few matches at half time, before their big men's matches just to give us a bit of publicity. They were great.

This was a time in which Socceroos' captain Johnny Warren and his brother Ross were at the Club. Frank Arok, who went on to become coach of the national men's team in 1983, had just begun his Australian coaching career with the club, so the women were in safe hands.

Ross was allocated the women as well, which was great. He was magnificent. He organised us uniforms and training fields. Fitted us in with the juniors and the older boys. They looked after us very well.

The St George Budapest women's team remained undefeated from 1971 through to 1977, and during the 1972 season they scored a total of 206 goals while holding the opposition teams scoreless. Added to their victorious run of titles while with Prague, the team had achieved a successful run of ten consecutive championships from 1967–1977.

During this time, the women's team dominated the NSW league with Pat as captain and Joe as coach. The team was to go on and produce players such as Julie Dolan, Cindy Heydon and Trixie Tagg, all of whom became State and National Hall of Fame recipients. Pat won the Golden Boot award each year she played and became a FFA Hall of Fame recipient herself in 2001.

By 1973 the MLSA competition consisted of 12 regular teams, culminating in a representative MLSA squad playing exhibition matches at the Bankstown Soccer Centre in conjunction with the semi-finals and finals of the commercial soccer competition for the men's teams. However, Pat is quick to point out that they didn't do this all on their own, and that all of those involved in the development of women's football in NSW should be remembered.

On the north side of the Harbour, women's soccer was being driven by the efforts of Leonie Parker, who had originally become involved because of her daughter's wishes to play and who couldn't understand why girls could not play football. Leonie formed Killarney Heights Ladies Soccer Club in 1974 and was instrumental in the creation of the Manly Warringah Women's Soccer Association.

In that first year we would play anywhere and anyone we could in the metropolitan area, but it was non-competitive at that stage and we wanted to play more serious soccer, and the travelling became too difficult. After two years I nearly gave up and had it not been for an impromptu meeting with Eric Worthington (Director of Coaching) at a barbeque we may have given up. He put me in touch with a lady named Jocelyn Eade, who was starting up the Ku-ring-gai District Association, and we ended up playing with them for a couple of years. We then decided to set up on our own and ended up with eight teams in the MWWSA. (Leonie Parker)

Women's football was also gathering momentum in the Eastern suburbs of Sydney. Kay Kress was instrumental in forming the area's first women's club team, the Rangers.

The first teams to compete in the Association included the Rangers, Sydney University, University of NSW, Pagewood, and Dover Heights Girls' High School.

In other parts of the State, the Macquarie and District Women's Soccer Association formerly ran Northern NSW before a Northern NSW State Association was formed in 1977. In the same year, the Metropolitan competition included Ku-ring-gai, Manly, Nepean, Eastern Suburbs, St George, Sutherland, Canterbury and Southwestern Districts, with more than 200 teams.

Women's football was also developing in other nations. Club teams usually limited to small local competitions were keen to explore playing opportunities overseas.

These teams did not require sanctions from any governing body to travel, so did so freely. In 1974, three teams from New Zealand visited NSW to play in a nine-day Australian Tournament against local club sides. Games were played at Wentworth Park, Englefield Stadium, and Bankstown Soccer Centre.

Pat and Joe organised the tour in conjunction with the New Zealand Northern Women's Football Association and, in particular, Secretary Jan Innes, who travelled with the teams to Australia.

They came to Sydney to play a tournament against three of our local sides. The New Zealand teams were Eden Saints, Papakura—East Coast Bays and Blockhouse Bay and, of course we were St. George Budapest then. The three Sydney teams were St. George Budapest, Blacktown Spurs and Ingleburn.

And St George won!

In February and March 1975, Blacktown Spurs and Ingleburn RSL, the latter coached by Jim Selby, returned the favour and visited New Zealand to play in the Air New Zealand Cup. They competed against leading club sides from Auckland, Blockhouse Bay, and Eden Saints, and teams from Hamilton, Whangarei, and Wainuiomate.

The Australian Women's Soccer Association

By 1974, regular women's competitions had been established in most states of Australia. However, the female players were becoming increasingly dissatisfied with the discriminatory treatment they were receiving from the male-dominated established Associations. They wanted to be recognised as serious footballers and for their sport to be afforded credibility.

In 1974 Oscar Mate from WA, along with Pat, conducted a campaign to gain a nationwide commitment for a national championship and a national women's association.

Pat recalls the moment that Oscar first got in touch.

In 1974 I received a letter from a guy called Oscar Mate, who was running the WA state team. He contacted me and said, "Because you're in Sydney, would you and Joe be able to organise a national competition and get as many teams from each state over there as possible?"

Oscar had heard about what we were doing in Sydney and he said, "Sydney is the hub at this point. We heard you were the most organised state at the moment. Could you do it?"

And we took on the challenge. Oscar said that he could organise a WA state team and bring it over, but there'd be no chance of everybody traveling to WA. Besides, they just didn't have the facilities or enough interest to do it.

He said it would be better if it was done from Sydney. So of course, Joe and I thought, "Crikey, this is big."

So we went to our Association: I reported to everyone what was happening because I was the Secretary, and they said, "well, if you two can organise it and get it started, we'd be happy."

Realising that this was the way forward, Pat and Joe set out to organise the first national women's soccer championships to be held in Australia. Throughout that year Pat, Joe, and Oscar established contact with all Associations known to have women's competitions. They also talked about another idea: a women's association.

All the teams we had in the Metropolitan Ladies' Soccer Association were asked if they could billet out players from the teams that were coming over from Interstate because no one had any money, they couldn't afford hotels. And our teams agreed to that. Each team would take as many players as they could. So that was organised and then we went to all the local soccer grounds looking for venues saying can we run a match at your field and on such and such a day? We planned it all out.

We contacted all the States and said, "Have you got a team that you can send?"

And that's how it started; we got it all organised. Funds were a problem of course. I think all of the clubs donated their grounds, and we had a little bit of money in the kitty from the Association. Not a lot. And of course, we had to organise trophies and whatever.

We had a meeting, and we got the State team going. This was done mainly because we knew we had to have an organizing body because 1974 was the first national championships in August. So, the New South Wales Association was only formed a few months before that, because that's what we had to do.

It was really the very beginning of everything. But we had to do it to get things going to get the first national championships on the way.

The New South Wales Women's Soccer Federation was formed in 1974 and included representatives from the MWSA, Ku-Ring-Gai District Association, and the Manly Warringah Women's Soccer Association. Pat was elected President with Leonie Parker as Vice President.

All the teams in the Metropolitan Ladies Soccer Association put players forward, and the team was picked from everyone in the Association. Joe was the coach and Jim Selby was the assistant and they got the team going. One or two of the other guys formed a little committee between them and went through the girls. They all knew each other's players and they chose a team.

Everyone was included, everyone could try out. You didn't have to be brilliant, you just came along and tried out from wherever. I mean, all along, we never left anyone out, good or bad players. You just came along—you got your chance and that was it. We had to be fair to everybody.

In August 1974, the first Australian National Women's championships were held in Sydney, with games being played in Granville, Bankstown, and Centennial Park. The St. George Budapest team, plus a few others, represented NSW. Western Australia was represented by a team dominated by players from the Morley Windmills club, while Victoria featured a combination of players from Greensborough and Melton. Finally, Macquarie and Districts represented Northern NSW with the Brisbane Junior Soccer Association for Queensland.

Joe and I got our committee together and organised the first Australian Women's Championships in Sydney and the teams competing were NSW, Northern NSW, Queensland, Victoria and WA.

Joe coached, and I was the captain, and we won the first tournament in New South Wales.

It was a busy time.

Towards the end of the competition, team officials met to discuss the establishment of an organisation to promote, foster and manage women's soccer in Australia. Oscar and Pat were awarded for their hard work in organising the championship and were elected as President and Secretary. Frank Clark from Queensland was elected as Vice-President and Jacqui Ager from Victoria as Treasurer. Clark later declined the position due to work commitments and nominated Elaine Watson from Queensland to be the first Vice-President. This was to be the beginning of Watson's 20-year commitment to AWSA.

In addition, Rale Rasic, the National men's coach at the time, was asked to be National Advisor, while Nick Bray from NSW was appointed Publicity Officer.

Elaine Watson's contribution to the development of the women's game cannot be understated. Her dedication, drive, and commitment to making women's football the best it could be led to acclaim. Her efforts, combined with her strong and unwavering manner, saw her often referred to as the matriarch of women's football in Australia.

The O'Connors' input, of course, was also immeasurable. The grand scope of all they achieved—from the creation of the MLSA, the NSW Ladies' Federation, to the first National Championships, to their coaching accreditations and international club tournaments—all leading up to those first Matildas abroad in the 1975 Asian Women's Cup, are what truly make them the godparents of the game.

Under Joe's coaching and Pat's captaincy, NSW won the inaugural 1974 National Championship and followed up with victories in 1976 and 1977.

In addition to Pat's significant input as player and captain, Joe's contribution to the development of women's football cannot be ignored. All who played under Joe regard him as one of the greatest influences on their individual successes, and the growth of the women's game. Interviews with those women players mention him time and time again with the highest praise.

The first AFC Asian Women's Cup was held in Hong Kong from August 25 to 3 September 1975 under the tournament's original name, the Asian Cup Ladies' Football Tournament. Six teams competed, including Australia, Hong Kong, Malaysia, New Zealand, Singapore and Thailand.

The Asian Ladies Football Confederation (ALFC)

Before we can move onto the role that the 1975ers truly played in the inaugural Women's Asian Cup, it is important to gain an understanding of the status of women's football on the Asian continent in the 1970s. The unique relationships between major parties were paramount in the rapid growth of the women's game and led to Asia emerging as a leading region in women's football at that time. This is demonstrated in the lead up to, and creation of, the ALFC.

Asia has played a pioneering role in the development of women's football, most notably since the 1970s. The traditional approach to women's football in most countries, including Australia, varied from outright discrimination and bans to cautious support. While the governing bodies were largely concerned with the men's game and did not welcome separate organisations for women's football, particularly in Europe, the existing organisation for men's football in Asia, the Asian Football Confederation (AFC), saw no issue with a separate body to develop the women's game.

So, in 1968, the Asian Ladies' Football Confederation (ALFC) was formed with representatives from Malaysia, Singapore, the Republic of China (Chinese Taiwan), and Hong Kong. Its first elected President was Tun Sharifah Rodziah, wife of the former Prime Minister of Malaysia, Tunku Abdul Rahman, while Mrs. Veronica Chiu Chan from Hong Kong was elected Vice-President. She, along with husband Dr Chiu But York (Honorary Life President of the ALFC and long-time Vice-President at Hong Kong FA), played a major role in the running of the first Women's Asian Cup tournament in 1975.

More importantly it was the intimate connections between the AFC and the ALFC that was central to the smooth growth of women's football during this time in Asia.

While the ALFC was operated separately from the AFC, strong links between the two helps explain the successful launch of the Asian Women's Cup. The

AFC were aware of the ALFC and its projects because the people involved were intimately connected. Apart from Pat being elected as the third Vice-President in 1974, the entire ALFC board (members and life members) was either married to or directly connected to someone in the AFC leadership. So, the connection was naturally close during 1975.

Even if women's football was not a priority for the AFC, the overall situation in Asia was in contrast to the situation in Europe or Australia where the National Associations sought to actively control the women's game and the specific associations overseeing them.

However, it wasn't until 1974 that the Confederation began to meaningfully impact the development of the women's game in Asia. Veronica Chui Chan, Datin Teoh Chye Hin of Malaysia, and Charles Pereira from Singapore reinvigorated the organisation into action and led to the organisation of the first Asian Women's Cup in 1975. Coinciding with the United Nations International Women's Year in 1975 and the growing interest in women's liberation movements worldwide, the ALFC moved quickly and the foundations of the first Women's Asian Cup were laid by August 1975.

At an international level, FIFA played a waiting game, and only became involved in women's football when the ALFC returned to the scene in 1974 and began to organise competitions. FIFA, while not directly sanctioning the Women's Asian Cup, did support it indirectly through including information of the tournament in the AFC section of the FIFA News—a month after the event.

In Australia, women's football was growing rapidly but had still to reach the stage where State and National authorities had been formed. It wasn't until 1974 that the first national championship was held and the inaugural Australian Women's Soccer Association was formed.

The ALFC initially reached out to Pat and Joe in 1970:

> I had a contact from a guy called Charles Pereira who was secretary of the Women's Football Association of Singapore and he said they were trying to get the Asian Ladies' Football Association organised. And could he keep in touch with me? They kept trying to get this going and he fed me news now and again but nothing really happened for a while.
>
> He told me they were trying to get together a club competition and he said, "It's only just started, it's going take a few years, I'll keep in touch,"

and we did, we corresponded—we became good friends actually for quite a few years.

Pat was again contacted with the news that a competition was finally getting off the ground. AWSA gave permission for the NSW team to accept the invitation to the Asian Cup, which was to be held in Hong Kong in August 1975. At the same meeting it was also decided that AWSA would affiliate with the ALFC, and Pat was elected as the third Vice-President of the Confederation and served in that position for three years.

And then when it was all coming together, he contacted me and said they're trying to organise a club competition. And they were contacting clubs in the Asia-Pacific area to try and get club teams over there to play. "Would you bring St George?"

And I said, "Of course we would". And then, a little bit later on, he contacted me again and said, "it's not going be a club competition anymore, we've had a meeting of the Confederation and it's going to be a National League. Do you still want to come?"

I said, "Well, we can't, because we haven't got a national team at the moment."

Pereira said, "Well, can you field a team?" and I said, "Yeah, of course we can, but it won't be a national team."

He said, "OK, fine, get all your oks and you're welcome".

So we told everyone what was happening and no one complained.

No one put up any reasons why this couldn't happen, because there was no official national team and no Association at the time. Because it was 1974. We never did much about anything else. We had just got ourselves organised. So, he said, "If you can organise it with your national body, you can bring your team."

Prague had already been invited to the team competition when they had it organised, so he said, "Would you be allowed to still bring your team, because we'd like a representative from Australia to come over?"

Although we weren't a fully-fledged national team, Asia wanted us to be in our national colours. He said, "The other teams in the competition that you're playing against are organised. They have national teams, but this is fine as long as you can come over and play in your national colours, representing yourself and your country."

But Australia did not get the official invite to the 1975 Asian Women's Cup until early that same year.

Although The AWSA had given the NSW team permission to attend the tournament and at the same time affiliate with the ALSC, the governing authority in Australia at the time was the Australian Soccer Federation (ASF). The ASF started in 1961 and officially joined FIFA in 1963. FIFA only recognised one governing body, and in Australia in 1975 that was the ASF. Sir Arthur George was the President and Brian Le Fevre Secretary. As a representative of Australia, the team needed approval from the governing Soccer Federation as opposed to the AWSA, because they were not recognised by FIFA at that time.

A section of the ASF constitution stated, in part, that, *The National League, and/or its member clubs shall not arrange tours to countries outside Australia without first having obtained the consent of the Federation.*

And so Pat and Joe attended a meeting with the ASF held in Sydney in early 1975.

> That's when we contacted the Federation and Joe and I went to a meeting and we told them what the story was. We said, "Well, we haven't got a national team at the time, but it would be fantastic publicity for women's soccer and Australian soccer if we could go over there and be the first team to represent Australia in the national colours".

At this point in the history of women's football in Australia, the national women's Association was still in its infancy, having only completed the first national championships in August 1974. No national team had been selected, although the question was raised at the first meeting of AWSA as to whether a national team should be selected at the next national championships in 1975. However, the notion was defeated, as there was no expectation of Australia being involved in an international competition at that time.

Coincidentally at the same meeting, AWSA had given NSW permission to enter the Asian Cup.

We'd call ourselves an Australia XI. We wouldn't be the Australian national soccer team because there wasn't one. Of course, this was good for them at the time as well because they wanted to get into Asia. So, they said "Fine, fantastic."

The ASF gave Pat and Joe permission for the team to attend the Asian Cup as representatives of Australia, and as such were allowed to wear the green and gold playing strip with the Australian emblem attached. In 1974, NSW were the national champions and nine of the New South Wales players came from the St. George club.

Then we got our girls together and it was the St George team with Connie Burns and Sue Binns from Ingleburn. We got together, had meeting and said, "Well, you know, if we want this tour to go ahead, we've got to do some jolly hard work."

The Australian Soccer Federation, they were marvellous, said, "Fine— no problems." They helped us with the uniforms and everything. They said, "It's great that you're going over there. It's good publicity for you, and for us", and we got their blessings, so we had no problems.

While researching this section of the history, attempts to locate any written records of the above meeting and associated approvals given by the ASF proved fruitless. At the time, Pat was the Secretary to both the State and National Women's Soccer Associations, and all the minutes were meticulously kept in two different folders.

These were passed onto Noelene Stanley from NSW (Publicity Officer with the AWSA). However, they appear to have disappeared from the NSW Football headquarters in Parklea. In addition, it appears that all records associated with that time in the history of the women's game were lost. No one seems to know the reasons why.

They said there's no record of anything at all. No meeting records, no minutes, no nothing.

I just thought well, maybe because women's soccer wasn't really important at that time. They were keen enough to say to us "Well, OK, go ahead. It'll be good for Australian soccer and for women's soccer and everything". Maybe they just didn't bother recording it.

Once the official approval was given, the fundraising began in earnest. To Pat and Joe's surprise, the level of support was overwhelming.

> The girls all then said, "What about money?" and it was really brilliant because there was a millionaire family, and the lady was Mrs. Veronica Chiu in Hong Kong. And at that time, she owned the Lee Gardens Hotel in conjunction with her husband. Pereira said that all our accommodation would be provided, and the hotel is being opened for the soccer tournament. All the girls will be fed and transported to and from the games. The only thing you have to find is the fares.

The only downside to the tournament was that it was being held at the same time as the 1975 Australian National Championships, which were to be held in Brisbane. The absence of the NSW state team players provided a perfect opportunity for the other states to compete for the trophy. Western Australia was the eventual winner. And in response to a 1974 decision, the AWSA named the "All Stars" top eleven players from those championships in lieu of a National Team.

> Unfortunately, it was being held at the same time as the 1975 National Championships, so none of our girls could try out for the national team in 1975 because we were going to Asia.

Financial support for women in sport was virtually non-existent in the 1970s. While the ASF approved St George's participation in the Asian Cup, and assisted with the uniforms, they offered no monetary support. So, the women again relied on the support of community, family and friends. Most would not have been able to continue to play the game without the support of family and the wider community. Hard work and support were critical to keeping the women in touch with the football world. In this spirit, the fundraising for the required airfares began in earnest.

The girls all agreed, keen to go. We started organizing car washes and raffles, you know the usual things that everyone does to raise money.

The girls were great. The clubs were great.

All the men's soccer teams allowed us to go to their matches every weekend and we had white t shirts printed with each men's club soccer colours on the front and their badges. They allowed us to go around to all their matches every weekend and fill these T-shirts – whatever we made was ours. We did that every weekend.

St George Soccer Club organised functions at the club to help us raise money, and the Apia club were brilliant. They organised functions at their club as well.

At the time Archie Blue (Apia) organised some of the guys that were playing First Division at the time to play an exhibition match against the girls going to Asia. Obviously, we didn't win!

But you know they all chipped in—it was brilliant. Yeah, you name it, we did it, and we got there. We got the fares together. We had our own traveling uniforms, so we had green slacks and a gold and white striped top, which was in the national colours, which we supplied ourselves.

People and organisations were quick to provide whatever support the women needed to help raise the required funds.

I only had to contact people – like when we were going away, I physically went around to people like Pepsi and all the big companies to see if we could get a few bob towards the fares to take the team away.

The guy was lovely there and he said "Look at the moment we haven't got any funds we could donate, but what I'll do is, if you give me the details of your trip and where your hotel is, every day we'll get a delivery truck full of Pepsi delivered, crates of it every day, this is our donation." At that time, although we probably shouldn't have worried, everyone was worried about drinking the water in Asia. They said it was great, but we were a bit unsure.

We said to our girls, "Well, please don't eat salads, as they could be dirty from the water, because we didn't want anybody to be sick." And so, we said, "You want a drink? Just come to our room every day and take the drinks back to your room and you've got it there." It was advertising for them as well, which was brilliant.

Yeah, so that's more or less what we were doing all the time, sort of traveling around seeing what we could drum up in the form of help.

And of course, as always, the local newspaper was an amazing source for them.

And that's when I had a call from the Australian Soccer Pools, and we had put a little note in the paper saying we were about $1,500 short. So, the Australian Soccer Pools phoned me and said "Guess what? You just got your $1,500. We're going to donate it." You couldn't fault people—well I couldn't anyway. "Give us a little bit of publicity and we'll donate the $1,500. If we can take a few photos of you training or something, that'll be fine and we'll donate the money."

So, they came out to the training ground, took a few photos and the next thing I got the cheque! I never heard any more about photos or whatever, but they did donate that.

Everyone joined in the race to raise the necessary funds, and no stone was left unturned. Members of the team rallied around and put their heads together to come up with whatever it would take to raise the money needed.

And once they had the money – it was time to go!

Trixie

After Trixie joined the team in 1967, she stuck with Pat and Joe throughout the record-breaking run into the 1970s.

We were there for three years from 1967 to 1970. And then the whole team went across to St George Budapest. And we played at St George from 1970 till late 1977 or early 1978. I don't know the exact date. We were there for eight years.

It was during this time that AWSA was formed. Trixie explains that:

> If it wasn't for Joe and Pat O'Connor, the Australian Women's Soccer Association (AWSA) would not have happened. They were just unbelievable. They did everything—they went to so many meetings and organised so many different competitions. Furthermore, they took our team all over the place to get more experience, and to promote women's football.

She recalls a specific instance when the team was returning home after the 1974 FIFA Men's World Cup in Germany.

> We travelled by boat to Singapore and visited Charles Pereira. Pat and Joe suggested touching base with him, because he was keen on organizing an Australasian tournament. We had a lovely conversation. He said something about wanting to organise a tournament. When I came home from the 1974 World Cup, I found out that Pat and Joe had been contacted.

And of course, soon after that informal contact, the formal invitation was received for the team to represent Australia in Hong Kong. Trixie was heavily involved in the fundraising aspects of the arrangements as well as keenly aware of the delicate politics of the situation. She describes the whole scenario from her point of view:

> We had to get permission from the Australian Soccer Federation (ASF) because it became an international tournament. Pat and Joe explained to the full committee that we had received an invitation and that our touring party would have members of three clubs with the vast majority coming from St George.
>
> The ASF gave us permission to participate because NSW were the 1974 National Champions. Nine of the New South Wales players came from our club. And because we had been fundraising for so long, they gave us permission to wear the green and gold shirts with the embroidered Coat of Arms. Because the tournament was a tournament for countries, not clubs.

That's how it started, and people have to realise that. The invitations didn't give much time to put a squad together. It's totally different now, we have proper selection processes, scouts going around, and we have multiple age, state and national championships.

Nothing had been done at an international level until that period.

Trixie, like many of her teammates, emphasises that tournaments, national recognition, international play, and more, do not just pop up overnight.

People just don't understand that international tours had to start somewhere. The ASF were the ones in charge in Australia and they gave us their blessing. There was no money given to help us with the tour, but once we got that official permission, we were able to start fundraising activities—delivering phone books, car washes and rentals and organizing school dances. The list goes on.

But once we had the funds—off we went!

Christel

Christel played with Pat's team for three years at Prague and happily went along with them in the move to St. George in 1971. During her time playing football in Sydney, Christel returned to Germany a few times to visit family and to work to raise money. While she was there in 1974, she was selected to play for FC Bayern Munich, a German professional sports club based in Munich.

I came back to Australia and then I went back again because we wanted to have a big service station here but there wasn't enough money. To make money, you had to go back to Germany.

We went back and worked hard so we could come back to Australia and pick up a business here. We always went on holidays to Queensland, like from Sydney, and we went right up to Cooktown, to look at different businesses. And there was a beautiful big business and so we said, "All right we'll grab it," but we needed more money so that's why we always went back to Germany. While I was there, I also played soccer.

The ban on women playing football had been lifted four years prior, and now Christel was free to play in her homeland.

> When I was back in Germany in 1974, I played for Bayern Munich, in the girls' team and I trained with Beckenbauer and Miller. We trained on the same field not on the same team. They weren't as famous then. I even got paid for playing for Bayern Munich.
>
> At the end of the season, they usually say, "Look, don't call us, we'll call you", so if you're good enough they call you back, and you know, they called me back! But then I came back to Australia.

While on that trip back to Germany, Christel found out that the St George team were forming the basis of a squad to travel to Hong Kong.

> During this time, I went back to Germany a couple of times, but I always came into the team when I came back. On this particular trip to Germany, they said: "We're going to go to Hong Kong, so you have to come back"—so they called me back. I just left Germany and came back to train and be ready for Hong Kong.

Christel was working in Goldfield House as a security guard at the time, and while the team were always training hard, she knew that the social status of women's football meant money would be an issue. Like the others, she was heavily involved in the fundraising.

> Nobody expected to get paid, it was a social sport. We were invited to go, and Mrs Chui paid for the accommodation, but we still had to make the trip and it was quite expensive. So, we started running raffles, and at St George, we served food and then we helped cook in tournaments. You know, we were helping in the kitchen to make money, but then, I said "Look, we still can't reach our goal."

Fortunately, thanks to the help they received from outside sources, Christel was mistaken—much to her delight as she joined her team on the way to Hong Kong.

Gundy

Gundy followed in her father's footprints and was always interested in football. The drive to play led her meeting up with Pat and Joe O'Connor in 1971.

> I always wanted to play and then I thought that, if you want to do something, you should chase after it. St George Budapest was the big team in our District. I think Johnny Warren was playing there, Attila Abonyi, Manfred Schaeffer—lots of famous names.
>
> And so I thought I'd just ring up the club, and they said "Yeah, there's a women's team." They gave me the number of Pat and Joe O'Connor.
> I borrowed my dad's car and drove over there. Pat and Joe had a permanent football pitch in the backyard, so I just started playing there and went to winter training from then on. After that, I started playing with them in the St George Budapest team.

Gundy was 18 at the time and her father was happy to support her playing as long as she could get there by herself. Relying on family and friends was critical in keeping the women in touch with the football world.

> So, I used to arrange with someone to meet up at the railway station or a pick-up point if someone had a car. The Metropolitan Women's Soccer Association didn't have all that many teams at that stage, maybe 7–8 teams, and they were all over Sydney. So, we travelled everywhere.
> If I couldn't get a ride, Penshurst Park was right on the bus line. So I'd wait for the bus to come around the corner down Forest Rd and I jumped on the bus to come home. I lived at Strathfield then.
> I remember Julie Dolan—I used to pick her up from her home and take her to training, she must have been about 12 or something. I had a licence by then, so I used to pick her up. She was just starting then—kicking a ball around the backyard and somehow, she got in touch with Pat.

Most of the team training was done at Penshurst Park but getting selected to play was not an easy task. Joe was strict as a coach, and the senior players at St George were serious about the game, helping Gundy develop the skills she needed to play.

> I had to pass the test with Pat and Joe—I was pretty rough and ready but I hadn't really played soccer or anything. I didn't play with any team because as I said, my parents wouldn't take me anywhere. So suddenly I was old enough to get there myself.
>
> The good thing about soccer is that you can practise the skills on your own. I just practised with the ball against the wall. Joe always said that the best practice to start with is just kicking the ball against the wall close up.
>
> I didn't get an actual game for ages because you know Joe was pretty strict, you had to earn your place on the team. And there were too many good players on the team. So, I would go to the game and after the game, come back home—no I didn't get a game! That was a bit disappointing, but the training, we were training twice a week and it was just training, training.
>
> The more mistakes you make the more experience you're getting. To refine it, you have to make the mistakes to actually get better. I remember Joe saying at one time that by just kicking the ball to each other, you're not really learning anything, you're not improving your skills. You have to do drills to learn the skills.

Gundy eventually earned her position on the team with the help of the coach and her teammates.

> But even then, I would wonder: "I've got so much to learn here, so many mistakes to make." Like when you're young, you think you can play, you think you've got it. And then ten years later I realise I didn't know everything!
>
> You can't go past a mature player. Pat, Joe and Christel, Trixie was pretty young, but experienced and had a lot of skills. And they took the game seriously, that's what I loved about them. They took the game seriously. They respected the game and that's what I liked.

Gundy developed a strong connection with Joe, who had a major influence on her football career.

> Joe O'Connor was the only coach I ever had. He was the only influence, no one else. He's the only one who guided me the whole time and I remember saying to him, "I'm slow, I'm not fast" so I'd never be a striker, or even a midfielder, so I ended up in the backs.
> I like reading the game. I always said to myself, "Expect the unexpected". If there's a goal then this is a mistake that someone could have made up the front, but ultimately, it'll be blamed on the backs!
> So, I used to counteract speed with thinking. After every game I just go through the whole game in my mind, especially things that you have done wrong, so that you figure out what you should have done.

Rale Rasic, who was coaching at the St George club and was the National Men's coach until 1974, was a supporter of the women's game and had an impact on Gundy. As she puts it:

> I used to live at Leichhardt, and Lambert Park was down the road from me. I used to go and watch them train now and then, and Rale Rasic was the coach of Apia at the time. So, it was interesting just seeing the drills they were going through.
> Once, in 1974, he came and talked to the girls. And then, like I said, I'd go to Lambert Park and just watch training and look at him from a distance, from the stands, and listen to what he had to say and watch the players go through their drills.

Gundy stayed with St George throughout the 1970s and in 1975 represented her country at the inaugural Asian Women's Cup. Like the others, she recalls the enormous amount of fundraising undertaken by the team in order for them to actually get there.

> What I remember most is lots of fundraising activities!
> We played trial games. 1974 was the World Cup in Germany with Australia participating so it was a great era, great time for soccer in

Australia. We knew all the players and all the names because a lot of them were with St George, so they were household names. We played against a sort of mock up team of the men for a bit of publicity—it was a great thing.

Julie

It was already 1975 when Julie happened to meet Pat and Joe and join the team that would become the First Matildas.

By that time, I was playing state hockey and one of the women who was also in the squad, she took off to footy training one night. I thought, "Yeah, that sounds like me." So, the next week, I joined her, and hockey fell by the wayside.

St George Budapest were where all the legends were, Trixie Barry at the time, Joe and Pat O'Connor. So, I landed with my bum in the butter there!! Joe O'Connor, he was great. They'd basically set up the Metropolitan Ladies Soccer Association in 1968 and that sort of got things underway after everything stopped back in the 1920s.

Joe's influence was paramount in the development of the women players that came to the St George Budapest club. Julie reflects on Joe's contribution and her teammates to the development of her own game.

Joe didn't have an A license or anything like that, but his training sessions, they were the ones that had us playing against 18- and 19-year-old men in every session. I believe that's what made us a whole lot better. You know, we're playing against blokes with faster movements faster, stronger ability on the ball, and we were pitted against them every week so in terms of training we got some of the best back then.

Trixie, Pat and all those people back then were great mentors. They were great players in their time and you know to learn from them at 14 years old to be able to learn from people like that was really fortuitous for me. So, I believe that I had one of the best starts I could have in football. Of course, the year that Julie joined was a fortuitous whirlwind for her.

I was 14 when I went there and within a few months they decided to take me to Hong Kong with them. So that was, you know, it's just the timing of everything in women's football.

It was a massive undertaking really for my parents as well as me because believe it or not, people didn't pack their bags and get on international flights back then. It was a big deal with the organization, all the funds to be raised and finally getting on the plane.

I remember when people got on planes and landed in foreign countries everyone stood up and cheered because it was something that didn't happen very often, and people were still sort of uncertain about planes. There was a lot of clapping and a standing ovation when the pilot landed and especially at Hong Kong Airport, which, by all accounts, had the shortest runway in the world.

After being introduced to the game, the support of both community and family were crucial in keeping Julie and women like her involved and successful in the game.

In all of our careers, mine were the kind of parents that if you were going to follow that path, they would support you 100%. Yeah, so whatever paths we did choose, we knew that they were there to back us up. Mum particularly got involved with my career and that of my sister while she was playing, because it was an area where people needed help and she could provide that help as well.

For me, when we moved to Alstonville, I couldn't get back to Sydney to keep playing with St George unless mum and dad funded me. It was really important that people got behind everybody back then.

Support from fans, family, friends—it all meant the world to women footballers.

Kay

The meeting in 1974 with Pat and Joe sticks out in Kay's memory.

I waited until the game was finished and then spoke to Pat and Joe O'Connor, because they were the ones that really started football here in Sydney and probably in Australia.

I was talking to them about the soccer, and I didn't know the girls were playing soccer in Sydney. And then Joe said, "Well, we've only got five teams in Sydney, Manly, Blacktown, Ingleburn, and St George." And so then I said, "I'd love to play", and he said, "Well there's no club in the Eastern Suburbs."

I asked all my netball girls if they wanted to play soccer, and I took a team of netballers and arranged a friendly against one of the teams— Ingleburn. We played that game and we then decided, the girls decided they would like to continue. So, we said, "OK, we want to put our Eastern Suburbs team in your competition." We were called the Rangers, and that was the first team in the Eastern Suburbs.

And so, at that time every week we would go either to St George, Blacktown, Ingleburn or Manly to play.

1974 heralded the beginning of the Eastern Suburbs women's competition and in the following year, Kay was integral in the formation of the Eastern Suburbs Women's Soccer Association.

Then I decided to form the Eastern Suburbs Soccer Association, so I contacted the Universities and they said they'd like to put a team in. I got teams from Sydney University and the University of NSW. And then I asked the Pagewood Soccer Club if they were able to get a girls' team together. And they did. And then we had one high school put a team in.

We ended up with like five or six teams here in the Eastern Suburbs.

Women at the Minda Remand Centre and Silverwater Detention Centre also joined the ranks of women's soccer during this period. Kay, as President of Women in Sport Foundation, worked with the Department of Corrective Services to initiate the formation of women's soccer teams from within the two facilities as part of a recreational and a rebuilding program. The teams played against a number of established teams in the Metropolitan Association, with the women from Silverwater calling themselves Sydney United, eventually joining the Eastern Suburbs competition.

Perhaps moreso even than some of the others, Kay acutely felt the lack of moral, financial, or social support for women's football at the time.

> We got no support from anybody, no media coverage, no sponsorship or anything, and some of the fields we played on didn't even have a women's toilet. Astonishing because you would expect them to have toilets for spectators or something. We used to hire the ground in Centennial Park and the ground that had the soccer fields on it at that time didn't have a women's toilet. You had to walk halfway across the park to get to the toilet.

After playing in the Eastern Suburbs competition during the early 1970s, Kay and her husband Nick decided that they would travel outside Australia and investigate the possibility of playing teams in Asia. Nick was a referee and coach of the Eastern Suburbs Rangers at the time.

> After a couple of years of playing we thought that it would be nice to take a couple of teams to Indonesia and Singapore, because at this time we didn't know that they were interested in having the Asian tournament. We thought we would go and have a couple of friendly games with those people. We went to Indonesia and then to Singapore and we spoke to a Charles Pereira who told us about the Asian Women's tournament they were trying to organise.

Pereira introduced Kay and her husband to Veronica Chui in Hong Kong.

> We decided to go to Hong Kong and just have a chat with her about when they were going to do the Asian tournament and whether they were going to do it, and she basically organised everything. She owned the hotel we all stayed in. She organised all the teams; there was Thailand, Singapore, Hong Kong, Taipei and New Zealand. And they all stayed in her hotel. We didn't have to pay so she was really good.
> We then cancelled our club trip, which actually made my club very unhappy, but we couldn't afford to do both, so we just thought we better stick to doing the one thing. And at the time Joe and Pat were the leading coaches in women's soccer, especially Joe, he was a really good coach.

St George didn't lose a game for 10 years or something—unbelievable.

Nick was also involved in a number of fundraising activities for the team after they received approval to play.

My husband organised a curtain-raiser with the girls and one of the men's teams in Moore Park. I think it was Hellenic. We did a curtain-raiser there, but they didn't show it on TV.

But it was really funny. While the girls were playing, and I was sitting in the stand because I just had one of my babies and I'm sitting in the stands, and I can hear this crap above us when the men came on. They said, "bring back the girls!" They hadn't seen girls playing before, playing exciting soccer and scoring a lot of goals.

Kay and her husband Nick became part of the touring party, though Kay did not play—she acted as an organiser for the team. Nevertheless, she was still an important part of it.

Sue B

Being part of a sporting family, Sue was influenced by her brothers and was always keen on sports. Sue spent her youth playing netball with the Guildford Wanderers, until the club decided to introduce soccer. Sue started playing at the age of 13 in 1970.

I was always sporty, coming first or second in my age group in athletics throughout my high school years. I had a love of many sports, including soccer, basketball, netball and athletics.

When I lived in Coffs Harbour, I enjoyed being a tomboy and either played cricket or rugby with my father and brothers or went to watch the local rugby games. I played basketball at school at Coffs and when we moved to Sydney (I was halfway through year seven). I wanted to keep playing so I joined the local sporting club Guildford Wanderers thinking I had registered for basketball. I soon found out that I had joined a netball team, but I adjusted and loved the game.

> Then whilst at training, I noticed the club had a girls' soccer team, which I registered for as soon as I could. The team they had there was only social when I first started, but they got the competition going the next year. I just really loved the game and I played with them for quite a few years.
>
> I started netball first and that's how I found out about soccer, so I'm pretty sure I started soccer pretty much after that. It was 1969, so it had to be around 1970 I started playing soccer, I'm sure.

Sue's father first came to Australia from England as a teenager and had a love of football. He later became a policeman, which required the family to travel a lot during those early years with stints in Menindee and Coffs Harbour, before eventually moving back to settle in Sydney.

Without the influence and support of family, women often found it difficult to play in a male-dominated sport. In Sue's case, while her parents were not directly involved in her playing the game, they didn't restrict her desire to play and her father was often there to cheer her on.

> When I was brought up, female soccer wasn't taken seriously. However, Dad would come to local games and sometime away games to watch and spur me on, frequently providing his expert advice. He would often watch myself, or my brothers, playing soccer and always offered his 'suggestions' on how to play. He would yell at us from the sideline but that is probably the only time we wouldn't do what he told us to do, because he couldn't get to us. (Laughter)
>
> Soccer was in the family and Dad was English, so he really liked the game as well. We all played, my brothers played at the same time with the Wanderers club. My son also started soccer at that club.

While playing with Guildford, Sue's talents were noted and she was asked to join one of the leading metropolitan clubs at the time.

> I stayed in that team in Guildford and then Jim Selby asked me to play with the Inglewood RSL side. Ingleburn and Blacktown were strong sides in the metropolitan competition, although they always used to come

a close second or third behind St George who won the comp in Sydney all the time. Ingleburn and Blacktown were going over to New Zealand to play in the 'Air New Zealand Cup'.

During the 1970s women's teams were beginning to improve and grow in confidence and many wanted to spread their wings. This sometimes resulted in teams looking outside of the local competition. In early 1975 the respective coaches of the Ingleburn RSL and Blacktown Spurs teams, Jim Selby and Fred Turner were planning to visit New Zealand to play in the 'Air New Zealand Cup' against leading club sides from Auckland and Hamilton. The New Zealand teams had previously visited Australia in 1974, and the clubs were keen to revisit the competition.

Ingleburn won the competition beating the New Zealand teams and Blacktown. I played really well over there. So, I think the coach must have recommended me to Joe O'Connor to go to Hong Kong. It was pretty late in the year because I wasn't involved in any of the fundraising or planning of the trip.

I don't know whether the team had someone else that dropped out or not—I'm not too sure, but I was happy to be included.

Sue needed to make a decision. She had been told that she had a good chance of being picked in the State side to play in the National Championships, which were being held in Brisbane that year. But they would coincide with the Asian Women's Cup.

Jim said to me that the national championships were going to be played in Brisbane at the same time. Some people weren't happy because a lot of players were going to Hong Kong that may have been selected for the National team.

Kim

In 1970, a few family friends, via Kim's father, started her on the path that would eventually lead to Hong Kong and beyond.

> I got involved in women's soccer because of my father and two very good family friends, Scottish friends who helped create the Blacktown Workers Soccer Club.
>
> They coached and they wanted to create a women's soccer team. So, all the kids, including myself, were asked to join in and form a women's soccer team for the Blacktown Workers' Club. So that was my first team.

The tyranny of distance associated with playing soccer in the Metropolitan Association often required individual sacrifice in order for the players to stay involved. Kim was no different, as training when playing for St. George was held at Peakhurst Park in Hurstville.

> I used to stay at my grandparents' place during the week because they lived in Hurstville. It was too difficult to travel from the City to Blacktown after work and then traveling all the way up to Hurstville, and then come home because I also played netball and softball. I used to come home for the Saturday softball games or whatever and then go back for the Sunday soccer games, depending on where it was or where training was going to be.

It wasn't long before Pat and Joe O'Connor noticed Kim's soccer abilities, and as a result she was poached from Blacktown and moved to the star-studded St George Budapest side.

> I went to the tryouts for the first Australian championships in 1974 and I got selected for the NSW team. From there I got more involved with Pat and Joe and the St George girls, and they convinced me to move to the St George team. I believe it was at the end of the Championships I went to the St George team. It was the year that the girls were preparing for the 1975 tour that I actually started playing for St George.

Kim has many memories of the hectic preparations that the team made for the tournament.

The first challenge I faced was trying to get organised—time off work, and getting money together to pay for it all. Doing raffles, doing lamington drives, we did a "Soccerthon" down at Ingleburn. I remember that vividly because I tore the ligaments in my ankle. That was not long before the actual tour was going to be on, and we played soccer overnight. I can't remember how many hours we played for.

We also did a walkathon from the city to Cronulla Beach and raised money that way. We also did car washes. I also remember doing a lot of training. St. George training, of course—but we're still playing for State as well, so we did our St George training, our State training, and we still played our weekend games.

It was the excitement of going, the excitement of representing my country in a sport, wearing the green and gold. Just coming together and working as a group, a family, trying to make sure that we could all go.

And raising all the funds that we needed to raise.

The colours they wore, the training they did, and the way that everyone rallied around them—it truly was a national experience, a national team, and Kim was thrilled to be a part of it.

Lyn

The year was 1970 and Lyn was 18 years old when she met Trixie.

I studied at night and in the second year, because I actually took it over a three-year period, I met Trixie. And she said, "We play, you know, we do training and that," and I thought that training would be good because I hadn't been doing any exercise at all. And that's where I started. It was through Trixie, and we were training up at Penshurst Park.

Lyn started playing for the St George Budapest team in 1970.

Some of the other girls had, I think previously played with Prague, then they joined St George, and I just came in on that.

> We'd go out to Blacktown, to Glenfield, all over the place because in those days, there really wasn't the number of teams you have today and the number of players that you have now compared to what they were in those days is no comparison really.

Distance was their enemy, but Lyn and the others were innovative and found ways to keep themselves, and each other, going.

> It was just getting to places. I remember that a couple of times we even went to the northern beaches. Just getting there was, you know, hard enough. But then people that were able to transport you, would. You could share rides and things like that so that wasn't so bad.
>
> I was able to drive then, so I was able to drive out to the game. I had a little VW and I was able to drive out to the different venues and I would sometimes pick up some of the younger girls—like Cindy Heydon. Cindy was only young, and her parents were very involved, but sometimes they had other commitments so I would often pick her up and take her to the game or things like that.

The women who played with St George during these years often refer to the team as a family—they had the support of not only their blood families, but their extended player family, too.

> Most of the support came from the families, in particular there were the Larsens and the Coates and the Kohens, and they were always very supportive of everyone. It had such a nice family-orientated feeling about it.
>
> And with the later games that I played, it was actually more like a family there because it was my girls, my now son-in-law's sisters, and even his mum, and we all played together. So that was like a nice family thing.

While Lyn's parents were focussed on other sporting pursuits, they never restricted her access to playing.

> I just did it because I enjoyed it. No one said, "Oh, what are you doing

that for?" It was just what I did.

My mum didn't worry about it at all. She probably didn't have that much of an interest. I was old enough and she didn't drive or anything like that, so it wasn't as though she needed to take me to places. I could get to places on my own.

She really didn't say much about it at all. Because, as I said, it was more rugby league and other things [for them]. We lived at Sans Souci, we would go sailing and things like that. Football in general wasn't, I guess a priority for us. Yeah, not even the boys got involved in rugby league or anything like that—it was more like sailing or cricket.

Lyn's start to the game was not what she expected, however she learnt from the experience and stayed with St George throughout the 1970s until they moved to Marconi in 1978, the whole time under the influence of Pat and Joe.

I think with my first game I was nearly sent off because I tackled someone. I really didn't know what I did wrong. I mean, I was just running up beside them and sort of obviously didn't go for the ball. Took out the player, so…!

[Pat and Joe's] involvement in the game was basically from grassroots—they were really involved in it, and were really trying to promote it.

About the preparation up to the inaugural Asian Cup, Lyn says:

I just went with the flow, basically, so I wasn't involved in any of it. My understanding now is that Joe and Pat were involved and Kay de Bry—they were from the Eastern suburbs, and they knew people in the Asian Association, and that's how it came about.

It was just getting money together to go. We would do car washes. I remember one time we walked from basically Circular Quay to the Gap, and on the way, (not the young ones), but the older ones who could go into pubs—we'd go into pubs with a bucket saying, "Can you give us some donations?"

You know, so it was yeah, a rather long walk!

THE FIRST MATILDAS

Aunty Tarita

During her time with St George Budapest, Aunty Tarita recalls the influence that Pat and Joe O'Connor had on her, both in soccer and in life.

> Oh God, they were fabulous.
> Pat was a fabulous captain. And you can't take anything away from that woman, I admire her greatly. And as for Joe, I absolutely adore him. That man is the only man that put something in my life and that something will be in my life forever.
> I've always been put down and kicked about, and it's only because when you're an Aboriginal person and you're right in that colouring where you don't fit in with the blacks and you don't fit in with the whites—somehow you fall through the cracks. But we still got through.

Aunty Tarita was 31 years old with a young daughter, Petra, when the team received the invitation to Hong Kong. It caused trouble for her private life, but ultimately, she still made the decision to stay involved.

> I went with a bit of a heavy heart, because when I got back, my marriage was over. But when I was over there, I just kept my mind on playing. I was focused and I wanted to do a good thing because there's no way I ever wanted to let my coach down. He meant everything to me. He believed in me. And I've never had in my whole life from the day I was born, to now, have anyone believe in me like my coach did.

Sue

During her time at St. George, Sue played on the right wing and, after years of learning her skills from the likes of Trixie Tagg and Cindy Heydon, developed a strong right foot and a goal-scoring partnership with Pat O'Connor.

> I was on the wing, right wing up front. I was known back in those days to have one of the best crosses in the game. And Pat O'Connor scored many

off my crosses and yeah, I was pretty good on the wing. I was fast in those days!

And to gain the skills and the experience and to play with people like, Trixie Tagg, Pat and Joe O'Connor and Cindy Heydon, yeah, it was just the absolute best experience to be part of that.

Perhaps even more so than most women who struggled with distance in the infancy of women's football in Australia, Sue felt the pressure of trying to travel to play thanks to her age. However, she was just as game as the others to try!

I remember as a kid when we first started back in Sydney, you'd have to travel miles. Sunday was the day that you would make your day out because they didn't have freeways and motorways and everything back then, so me living in the Sutherland Shire and having to travel to Liverpool or out to Ingleburn, like they were an hour, hour and a half trip.

And so, we played our soccer, and then we'd make a day of it. Everybody stayed afterwards and the mums would make sandwiches and we all had a great time. We'd have fun with the other team afterwards. I remember one time we had to go all the way out to Nepean and we basically had to chase the cows off the soccer pitch before we even played. In that particular game, nobody wanted to do any slide tackles because of the cow droppings!

So, it's all those little memories that really made it such an enjoyable time of life.

The attitudes of some men towards women playing football during the formative years were, sadly, not always positive, which was very noticeable to Sue. She also remembers, though, the satisfaction of watching them change their minds.

A lot of the time you had guys laugh at us. We played a lot of opening matches before St George Men's, we'd be the curtain-raiser and there were guys there that were, you know, basically laughing at you.

But when you got out there and showed them what you could do and the skills that we had, they were laughing on the other side of their faces. They were basically shaking their heads when you walked off the field and telling us that, they had absolutely no idea that we could play the game as well as we did. It was an eye opener for a lot of males and females.

One of the little girls that used to play, her name was Kathy she was in the crowd watching the soccer and she said, "Mum, I want to play soccer. I want to go and play soccer with the girls". So, Kathy became part of our team.

It was very new in those days and people just didn't realise the skills that the girls had. You walk off the field and you felt like saying, "See, we can play soccer. There was no need to laugh at us."

In contrast to the male supporters, the male-dominated Sydney clubs Sue played with during her 15 years were always supportive of the women's teams. In particular, the support from some of the greats of the game, including Johnny Warren and Rale Rasic.

I remember we met Johnny Warren a couple of times, when he was with St George. I went along to a coaching camp with Rale Rasic. I was over 18 by then and I was driving but we'd been to a soccer camp. Trixie, Rale, and I sat up one night and we had a couple of ports together, you know, just talking soccer when everybody else had gone to bed. And it was just lovely. A cherished memory.

Rale's recognition of the girls and his support of women's soccer was great as well. And Johnny Warren always said we could play, and he was always giving us a pat on the back and saying, "Well played," and you know we'd come off that field. He said a couple of times, "I wish some of my boys had the drive and the fun and the excitement that you put into the game."

We'd always get positive feedback from them and they always allowed us to use their facilities, like the club to do fundraising and have our presentation nights and things like that. Always so thoughtful and supported the girls' game, definitely.

Sue turned 16 the same year the women played in Hong Kong. While Sue was not involved in how the team came to be representing Australia, she has strong memories of the fundraising the women had to do, and the fun they all had in raising the money needed to travel overseas.

The thing that sticks out in my mind was all the fundraising and everything that we did and how all the parents and everybody got involved. We had lamington sales. We did walkathons. We did car washes. One of the girls, Christel worked at a petrol station, and we ran car washes on the weekend.

We had fundraising events, like we might have what they call a casino night or a card night, so we were always out there raising as much money as we could. St George got behind us on a couple of occasions where we were allowed to have functions at the club. Being underage, we couldn't go into the actual club itself, but we'd have these fundraising events where we might go around and sell raffle tickets and all that sort of stuff.

I think it was the fact that we had so much fun in doing that, knowing that in the end the results were going to be—you know—a trip overseas.

On top of raising the necessary funds, the women had to train hard to prepare themselves for the playing conditions they would face in Hong Kong.

We had a fitness trainer, Trixie's ex-husband, Kevin. And he was in the Navy, so he was our PT instructor. And I do remember the fitness training and the hard regime that we had before we went away, we knew we were going to be pushed, and we knew it was going to be hot and we would have to be fit.

Certainly, it was an aspect that none of the women would soon forget.

Vickie

Vickie met Pat and Joe in 1970 at one of her brother's football games.

I went to one of Kim's games and at half time I was kicking a ball around on the field, kicking it up in the air and trapping it, taking shots at goal and that sort of stuff, and Pat and Joe were there. And that was the beginning of my life in soccer really. They saw me and then they just came over to me and said, "Do you play soccer?"

And I said, "Well, no but I'd really like to, but there aren't any girls' teams", and they said, "Well, yeah there is."

So that was the moment of excitement, I think. I was about 14 or 15. I conned one of my neighbours into joining as well. But she wasn't nearly as soccer-oriented as I was. It opened my eyes that there were women playing soccer.

Vickie began her soccer career with all-conquering St George Budapest in 1970 and developed into a strong midfield player. She stayed with the team throughout their unbeaten run in the 1970s, much of which she attributes to the influence of Pat and Joe.

I was in centre midfield and played that position for a good proportion of my playing time until as I got older, I sort of moved back into the centre fullback position. I was the free kick taker and usually took the goal kicks as well.

I wasn't one of those people that would score goals from the forward line. I would score goals from outside the penalty box because I was quite strong. I also often scored through headers from corners taken by our wingers.

Once I started with St George I basically stayed there. I stayed on after Pat and Joe left and played under Alan Lytton as well. By that time, I was pretty entrenched in the team and we were a fairly close-knit group really.

And I don't think there was really much opportunity, well, there probably was opportunity, but I had no desire to change clubs or live anywhere else. I was really competitive, and at the time they were the best team anywhere. As a club team, we probably could have beaten any team in the country. It wasn't very long before I started playing State soccer. It just went from there, really. We didn't lose a game for many years, and we didn't let a goal in for many years.

I was obsessed. Absolutely loved the game. Absolutely loved playing. Idolised Pat and Joe and all the stuff that they could teach me. It was just like "Well, I can really do this now."

I loved training. My brother used to come to training with us. I think he used to learn more training with us than anywhere else really, which is pretty cool. So, it was a really exciting time.

Vickie, like everyone else on the team, has quite a few memories of the invitation and lead up to the Hong Kong tournament.

> It was pretty exciting when we had the chance to go. We were super excited, but we had to do everything for ourselves, we had to raise enough money to get ourselves there. I know that people were always out looking for sponsors and stuff and we were trying to get shoes or tracksuits or whatever we could find to take with us.
>
> But I wasn't part of any of the organizing stuff, so I don't really know much about what happened at the top end. We spent all of our time doing fundraising activities—everything you could think of, you know car washes, walkathons and raffles, and anything that we could do to raise money to help us get to Hong Kong. It was still such a novelty really that we even had the opportunity to go, I think.
>
> The first Asian Cup that was pretty exciting. It was clearly a highlight because nothing like that had happened before, so the fact that we had a chance to go and compete for our country, travel overseas and see what other people were doing and see how well they could play and how we compared to them. That's pretty cool.
>
> We were hopeful that we would be competitive and we thought at the time that we probably *deserved* to be there, because we were clearly the best. That's how we felt anyway.

The First Matildas?

There have been claims from different club sides as to who was the first ladies' team to travel and play overseas. Wynnum (Brisbane) women's team, who began playing in 1975, travelled to New Zealand to play for the Union Travel Trophy at the end of their first season. The Wynnum Club believes that they were the first club team to travel overseas. In 1977, Western Australia organised a tour of state players to Malaysia, and a regional women's team from WA also travelled to the 1980 Asian Women's Cup in India.

But Pat and Joe were the main driving force behind the growth of women's soccer in NSW during the 1960s and 1970s, combining to propel the women's game from a "kick and giggle" affair to the development of formal State and National championships. Pat looks back on it all with pride.

> St George was the dream team, every single one of those girls were great. Joe and I were involved in trying to organise everything through the years. We never had one ounce of problems and we went through ten years in Sydney. And you can add that our team never lost a match—ever—in that time. The girls were brilliant, and it was really terrific to be called the godmother and godfather of women's soccer by all those players.
>
> We just loved every one of them—still do.

Nick and Kay de Bry visiting Jakarta as part of planning for the tournament.

Christel Abenthum and Trudy Fischer model the Australian strip to be worn in the tournament.

Press conference at Sydney Airport on departure with Eric Worthington, then National Technical Director of the Australian Soccer Federation (seated), and Brian LeFevre, General Secretary of the ASF (standing).

Team photo leaving Sydney Airport, August 1975.

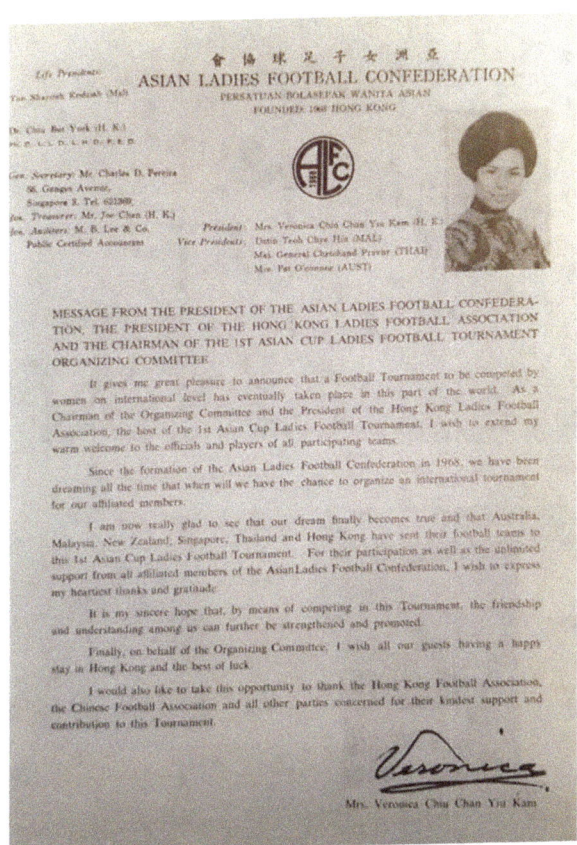

Welcome letter from the Asian Ladies Football Confederation Chairman.

Arriving at Hong Kong Airport, August 1975.

At the Opening Ceremony.

The jersey, flag and program used at the tournament.

(L-R) Trixie Tagg, Sue Binns and Lyn McKenzie at Sydney Airport on return from the tournament.

The late Joe O'Connor and Pat O'Connor in Perth, 2020.

A reunion in 2020 with (from L-R) Gundy Zarins, Trixie Tagg, Cindy Heydon, Rale Rasic, Christel Abenthum, Lyn Everett-Miller, and Trudy Fisher.

Asian Football Confederation – Activities in Asia

by Dato' Teoh Chye Hin
General Secretary of AFC, Ipoh, Malaysia

Tournaments in Asia

The year 1975 is a very busy one for Asia. We have so many events throughout the year that some National Associations are finding it difficult to cope especially when they also have their own national tournaments to organise.

The following are the major tournaments involved:

1. Pre-Olympic Preliminary Tournaments in Asia

Three Groups are being held to determine the three places for the Olympics Final Round in Montreal.

Ladies' Football

This being Women's International Year and on the initiative of the Hong Kong Ladies Football Confederation led by the energetic Mrs. Veronica Chiu, its President, the 1st Asian Ladies Cup Football Tournament was organised in Hong Kong from 25 August to 3 September 1975. Six teams, Australia, Hong Kong, Malaysia, New Zealand, Singapore and Thailand participated. New Zealand emerged champions with Thailand runners-up.

The organisation has great ambitions and they planned to send a team to tour Europe in 1976, that is, if a sponsor or sponsors could be found to sponsor the tour.

Asian Schools Soccer Championship

School Authorities in the East Asian Region have been organising annual tourna-

The FIFA newsletter of October 1975 refers to the six national teams represented at the first Asian Ladies Cup Football Tournament (courtesy the AFC).

Part 3
THE 1975ERS
Pat

The AFC Women's Cup arrived as a high-profile event. The teams and delegations from all over stayed at the recently built three-star Intercontinental Lee Gardens Hotel, towering as the highest building on the skyline at that time. All the teams had arrived by the 23rd of August, 1975, and were introduced to the media at a full press conference. The tournament was run by a 16-person committee made up of seven women and nine men, representatives from each team, and chaired by Veronica Chui Chan.

The opening ceremony was held at the Hong Kong Government Stadium on the 25th. All teams marched into the Stadium in the warm rain of the Hong Kong summer with the police band playing behind them.

Pat recalls the trip and the opening ceremony with nothing short of wonder.

Oh, goodness. It was absolutely brilliant. When we arrived in Hong Kong, coaches were waiting to take us to our hotels. Beautiful. We were ushered to our rooms, and we organised, you know, that there were so many girls to a room. Absolutely brilliant.

We were bussed in beautiful coaches to the ground. I guess they were trying to, you know, look after us, put on a good show. The military were there. They had their guns across their chests. We marched in between these soldiers and there were hundreds of fans outside the ground. They marched us through and into the grounds and we played in what was then the Hong Kong Stadium—massive place and truly, every match—it was full.

We had fans everywhere. I mean we were really chuffed because

> we were being asked for our autographs, you know—it made us feel really good.
>
> The girls went everywhere, there was no stone left unturned. If ever we wanted anything, we just had to ask. There were coaches if you would like to go to the zoo or whatever. Off you go, get on the coach, and you'll be taken and brought back. Yeah, absolutely brilliant.

As well as the reception and the way they spent their time, the football amenities were also remarkable to Pat.

> They had their training grounds all organised. Floodlights if we needed them. To play at the Hong Kong stadium was absolutely brilliant. At that stage in women's soccer, it really was fantastic. It was so well done.

Even more fascinating to her was the unexpected prestige that met Pat and her team in Hong Kong.

> Mrs. Chui organised Chinese banquets on the top floor of the hotel. Very often during the time we were there, Joe and I were invited to the top table, and we'd sit there on either side. Everyone on the table was an army general or somebody in the top ranks in Hong Kong, because at that time the military were there, not to shoot anybody or anything, but as a presence, just to make it look good.
>
> These guys were really fantastic, and this fellow sat next to me—he was a big man and we had 22 courses of this Chinese meal—all different things. And he said—he always called me Mrs. Patricia—and he said, "Mrs. Patricia, sometimes I will tell you not to eat something because it may not be your type of food."
>
> The different waiters would come around and he would say, "Mrs. Patricia I wouldn't eat any of that if I was you. I don't think that would suit your taste."
>
> Everywhere we went the military were there to look after us. It's not relevant, but it was so funny.
>
> The people that were organizing the tournament, the Asian Committee were brilliant, absolutely, for their first tournament.

THE FIRST MATILDAS

The competition was divided into two groups, Group A included Thailand, Australia, and Singapore, while Group B consisted of New Zealand, Malaysia, and Hong Kong. Group games were played as double-headers, with the first between New Zealand and hosts Hong Kong followed by Australia against Thailand.

Pat recalls those first steps onto the grass in Hong Kong—including the unexpected downside that the team brought with them.

> We got our gear on before the match and we'd seen the guys do it, so a few of us went out and walked around the ground and checked the grass. We walked to the goals, checked the nets and made ourselves look very professional and we enjoyed every minute of it!
>
> It was unfortunate that, as we arrived there, four of us had the flu, which we didn't know, nobody knew. I think one of our girls had it when she was going over and three or more of us got it and which was unfortunate, but we didn't let it make any difference to us. We carried on playing.

While New Zealand proved too strong for the host team, winning their opening match, according to the tournament report, the underdogs Thailand surprised the much-favoured Australian eleven by defeating them 3-2 in their opening group game.

> The other teams were great. I mean everything went well. We did get a bit of time to do some shopping and that. Hong Kong was super. There were no problems there and it was a great tour.
>
> And that was really the start of the Asian competition for women's soccer. I think it has carried on since then and obviously they still play there. So, I think we laid a bit of groundwork there for women's soccer as well. I have a feeling that at that time, the men weren't going to Asia very often.
>
> We felt that we had done something for soccer in general. Going over there, I tell you, the girls wore those uniforms with pride. You've never seen a bunch of girls so proud of their country. They were all fantastic.

Pat does carry one *what if* with her—the chance she *almost* had to become the first Australian woman to score in an international tournament. Had she scored the goal, it could have changed the course of the whole event, a fact she is keenly aware of. Nevertheless, she remembers the moment fondly.

> I think it was Trixie, what a ball, a cross from the corner. Over it comes, landed on my left boot, a superior pass, and I hit it with everything I had. And this is shortly after the game started and for some reason, I don't know where Thailand got this little goalkeeper from, she was dynamite. And I hit this ball from in front of the goal as hard as I could. And you know she dived over and saved it!
>
> I'm not bragging from my point of view, but I thought I'd scored. I hit it so hard. The pass was beautiful. I just said that's the first goal. But when I hit it, she dives across the goal and saves it!
>
> I always say to myself, "maybe that would have changed the whole tournament."
>
> You don't have a choice when a beautiful ball like that comes over, you haven't got time to put it anywhere in the goal, you just hit it. I still say to myself, "No, no, I didn't really have time to put it in the corner or wherever". I just had to hit it and I said in my head, "Great, that's the first goal."
>
> And she's only little this girl. I thought that could have changed the whole tournament, but as I said, you've got to hand it to her.
>
> You remember the goals you missed just as much as the ones you score, I think.

Australia may have lost the opening match, but the team went on to win the remaining group game against Singapore, 3–0, with Trixie opening the scoring for Australia in front of a reported crowd of 2,226 fans.

Pat and Julie Dolan also scored to help Australia finish second in their group… now into the semi-finals against New Zealand: it was a hard-fought match in front of 7,000 spectators, but Australia lost 3–2 in the end, with a goal each from Trixie and Julie.

The last double header of the event was held on the 2nd of September with a record crowd approaching 12,000 attending the playoff match for third between Australia and Malaysia. This time, Australia won 5–0, securing the bronze medal. New Zealand then proved too strong for Thailand in the final, winning the tournament 3–1.

After the tournament ended, a select group of players from each team were awarded an Asian All Stars badge. The plan was to send these players on a tour of Europe, but this plan never eventuated.

From Australia, those selected were Trixie, Julie, Connie, Christel – and, of course, Pat!

Trixie

Landing in Hong Kong was a life-changing moment for Trixie. No matter how much she'd thought about it beforehand, she was still overwhelmed by the honour of representing her country, the spectacle of the event, and how difficult the games were. The playing times were also a surprise, as the tournament allocated only 60 minutes per match, while the teams were used to playing a full 90 minutes.

Incidentally, this time difference was later used as one reason why the tour should not be recognised as a true international competition. As such, it became another purported reason why the 1975ers were not formally recognised as being part of a national representative squad.

Trixie recalls:

It was just an amazing experience. They were just so welcoming.

We were all very excited and didn't know what to expect. The very first day at the tournament, there was a torrential downpour, monsoonal rain. And we had to play in that!

In hindsight, I don't think we realised that the games were going be 30 minutes each half. I think that caught us by surprise, and we were lucky, I think to only lose 3–2. I think it was three nil down at one stage. But we managed to get two goals back. We ended up coming third in that tournament.

It wasn't just the visitors who were enthralled, though. Locals from Hong Kong got behind the tournament and turned out in large numbers to watch the games.

> Lots more spectators than we were used to, even though it rained a lot. On one side there was a covered grandstand and all the people that came were huddled under that.
>
> There's one photo where I'm in front of the goal, tapping into the goal, and you can see how many people there were. Apparently, the official figure is 12,000. We were only ever used to playing maybe in front of 200 people at the National championships in 1974! At club games we were lucky if we had more than 50 people.
>
> So that was probably the main thing I remember. But it was hard going. There was mud on the field, and we were excited. It was a big occasion for us.

Trixie played up front for the team and recalls the attacking combination that was so successful throughout their years together.

> Nowadays they call us strikers. But I was told that I was an attacking midfielder but yes, I did play a lot up front. And I'd be in the middle, Christel on the left wing, and I think Susie (Larsen) was on the right.
>
> Actually, I've got to thank Christel too. She helped me when I first joined the Prague team and we became very, very good friends. She learned all her football playing with some big names in Austria. Christel and I actually trained with men's teams a few times.
>
> She had a left foot I reckon that a lot of Socceroos would be jealous of. She was able to take a corner and put it in the top back of the net. Her left foot was unbelievable. A really good player.
>
> She was also one of the ones that were awarded an Asian gold medal. I've still got mine.

Trixie has no ambiguity over the role of her team, regardless of decisions and recognition by FA officials. In her own words:

> I think we can be proud that we sort of started the journey for international women's football in Australia.

THE FIRST MATILDAS

Christel

While Christel's memory of the games themselves is not so strong, she played in all three cup matches alongside the team. And even though she doesn't remember the specifics, she has strong associations with the formidable team she and the others made.

I'm a striker. I just score the goals.

Trudy was forward defence. Stacey would kick the ball into the middle to Trixie, who would pass it on to Pat or me to score. There was no going backwards, like we do now. I'd give it back to the goalkeeper and then we start off again. From the goalkeeper into the midfield and then up front—score!

That was our style and we kicked it hard. I mean, it's like the girls would say, "Oh you can't kick the ball so hard, you're scoring like a man". I said, "When you kick the ball, why not hit it hard so it goes into the back of the net?"

One of the significant issues from the Hong Kong event that Christel *does* remember clearly is the unexpectedly huge impact that the weather conditions had upon her and her teammates – not to mention other players and teams.

When we got there, we were totally fit. I mean, we had a fitness instructor, and we were coached to play the best. But the environment and then the different foods and probably the water affected us, we started to get colds and then we had the runs.

You have to cope with the climate—we didn't know what hit us. The humidity and the downpour of rain…we played, and then we'd go into the air-conditioned hotels…we weren't used to all this.

After two or three days we were all sick. Not to find excuses, but we are all fairly tall, and the Asian players were tiny, so as soon as we lifted our legs to kick a highball, we got penalties against us. And when we played, they just fell over because we're strong and they were so weak that we couldn't actually play a strong game.

The New Zealand team, though, didn't seem to have this problem.

> The New Zealand team, they just knocked them over and scored the goals and they won. When New Zealand used to come to Sydney, we beat them one time 10 nil, because we were equally as strong.
>
> But in Hong Kong, we tried not to be so forceful. And that was a bit negative in a way that we didn't win.

Despite not winning the tournament, Christel's experience of the Asian Cup stuck with her, particularly the novelty of playing in front of the much larger crowds. It was another experience that the players were not used to—that, and of course losing was not something the team had *ever* had to contend with until now!

> The experience itself, like to play in front of thousands of people, that's overwhelming. When we played in Sydney, we just had our own families there or like a few friends. Sometimes we just had a game before the men, but even in the men's game they got about 2,000 people. We usually had about 100 watching us, but there were 10,000 or more and they were hanging around the stadium to watch the games. That's something you have to get used to, you know, to have all that publicity.
>
> We also had to get used to losing matches, because we were always winning. Like when we go on the field we would say, "How many goals will we score today?" So that was a learning curve as well.
>
> I just hope we were good ambassadors, for the next generation.

Christel is under no illusions that there was any accident in how the 1975ers were not recognised as true representatives of Australian women's football despite placing a respectable third in an unequivocally international tournament. She believes politics based on the origins of the players had much to do with it.

> We called ourselves an Australian eleven, But I was not an Australian, so maybe they said—I mean it was never said out loud—"Oh well if you're not an Australian you can't call yourself an Australian."
>
> I was not naturalised at the time. The only reason I didn't become

naturalised is that, if I did, I would have lost my German pension.

I was all for Australia, I liked Australia. I wanted to stay. It's not that I wasn't sure where I belonged, but I think they had enough trouble getting the men's team going.

But they should recognise us. It would be nice to have this recognition—it had to start somewhere. And I'm proud to be part of the beginning.

[Modern Matildas like] Mary (Fowler) wouldn't be playing the game here, she wouldn't have come out of this, if it wasn't for the pioneers.

Gundy

While she only played in the first game against Thailand, Gundy was very much part of the team. She recalls especially the quality of the opposition and how hard it was for her own team to compete. She was used to being part of a squad so used to winning—suddenly their play did not always result in success. Third place is very respectable for sure, but Gundy believes they could have done better.

I do remember that I was dropped after the first game. I remember that well! I only played in the first game.

It's a different world out there, you know, top athletes. They were beyond normal, really extreme. We had a great team, and we came third in the end, which is very good. We were under constant pressure throughout the games, and I think we did pretty well. [but] It was very close, and we could have won it.

Gundy still believes that the 1975 tour and her team's place in it were not only an important part of football history, but a landmark moment for the women's sport in Australia overall—and that her team was a true Australian national team.

The 1975 tour to Hong Kong, you know the players really deserved it. It was a wonderful team and they got to show how they could compete with other national teams. We came third and could have easily won it.

We represented Australia. Everyone who saw that team said, "There's the Australian team," and we were recognised as the Australian team.

> If you're looking at paperwork or to tick a box, the fact is that we represented Australia and we played against national teams, and they got caps playing against us.
>
> So, if we're not the national team then they should forfeit their caps having played against us. I think everyone who played there deserves to be recognised as such. Everyone who played against us got a cap so obviously they recognise themselves as being deserving.
>
> According to the papers we went to Hong Kong as an Australian team. We played in the stadium as Australia versus New Zealand, Malaysia, or Thailand. What more can you say?

The fact that other teams in the tournament won international caps is a sticking point for Gundy and many others, both those involved in the event and fans who believe the 1975ers truly deserve recognition. After all, what was so different about their team that they should be left out? As we have seen, the answer remains unclear.

Gundy also tackles another common argument against them and cleanly rebuts it.

> If the argument is that it wasn't a true selected team, I'll tell you that it doesn't matter what team you pick. There will always be players who reckon they should have been picked. There will always be better players left out than others.
>
> The Australian Soccer Federation at the time had given their approval. We didn't go underhand, and we definitely wouldn't have gone without approval.

For the 1975ers, their experience in Hong Kong was not focused on the win or the loss, but rather the chance to represent their country and to play together as a team. Gundy reflects on why, exactly, the tournament was so important, both to her as an individual and her team, and also to women's football in Australia overall.

> Going through difficult things together is something—it doesn't matter what it is, like playing against international teams or another national

team. You know it's hard, you have to stand up, be counted, and play for each other and help each other. You've gone through difficult things and it's something that you just can't buy.

And when you go back to something, it's not as stressful, you actually have that extra experience. It's a bit like with club players; they don't like releasing players to the national teams. But you know the experience you get playing against national teams, you go back to the club, and you can't buy that experience or pressure.

The great thing I remember is the wonderful girls and great friendships especially. Playing other teams and the fact that everyone was playing the game they loved and respected.

All the girls, especially in the 70s—great players. A lot of fun.

Julie

The biggest impact of Hong Kong on Julie was the level of support shown by the locals—crowds which way surpassed any that the team were used to playing in front of back home—and the level of sport and gameplay that was unlike anything her team had experienced before.

The facilities were fantastic, everything laid on and not a thing out of place. Everything was timed to the minute. Our hotel, I guess it was four or five-star back then. I'd never been in an international hotel before. It was just comfy. All the food was laid on, training, transport as well.

Just being in a stadium, there weren't that many people there, but a lot more than we'd ever seen at a women's football game. And also coming up against foreign teams who were much quicker, much sharper. That's the kind of competition they played in their countries, whomever they played against, and I kind of understood then that things were at a different level. We hadn't been exposed to anything like that, so we were pretty much entering new territory there.

The other Asian teams were very fast, very quick, nothing that we'd seen before. It was a matter of getting used to that very quickly and trying to still play the game that we play.

All I remember is that the teams were a lot quicker than us, faster ball movement. It was just a matter of competing against a different kind of opposition and doing the best that we could. I remember that in all the games.

The biggest part of the process for Julie was realizing that it was like nothing she'd known before—probably nothing any Australian women's team had known before.

For me, I didn't know what to expect, so nothing really surprised me. I was like everybody else, I wasn't happy that we got beaten and thought, "This is a change." But that only increases your desire to go back and get better because you realise that no, you're not the best. You may have won everything for 10 years in your home country, but that means nothing.

And the fact of the matter was that, recognised or not, the 1975ers' journey was the first drop in what would soon be a broken dam. International travel in the 1970s became a popular alternative for women's teams keen to test their abilities and improve their games.

People were starting to travel. We were finding games overseas and because international travel was becoming a bit more accessible, I guess, then people got together with these players from overseas and organised tournaments, and that's the way it happened.

People at the grassroots were organizing things for themselves and there was no governing body that was really organizing things outside of the national championships. A lot of the time back then, like I said, people just travelled and took teams with them.

Because people were really keen to compete against others. And as I said, nothing was officially being organised, and also these pioneers were so used to organizing things themselves, because that's all they've ever done to get things started. So, we had an incredible number of people back then who were just really instrumental in getting the game going, pushing the game forward.

Pioneers of football, every one—and the First Matildas were in the heart of it all.

Kay

While Kay didn't play in Hong Kong, she enjoyed being part of the squad, particularly after being involved in the early days of organising. One of her strongest memories was the strength of the Thai team in Australian's opening match, especially compared to the Australians who had suffered something of a handicap.

> I was part of the squad, but I was the organiser, and I didn't actually play. Because they had enough players and they were better than me!
>
> On the trip over in the plane, most of the girls were really young and had never been on a plane before. We had like three or four of them get food poisoning on the plane. So, then they went out for the first game and we had a depleted team.
>
> They played Thailand. The Thai girls had a really good build up. The King of Thailand actually hosted the team at the palace and organised a camp for them there and looked after them. And then they all came in their really nice uniforms. Marching off the plane with a big banner and everything.
>
> They looked like a real army, and they were pretty impressive. We went to meet the other teams coming off the plane, and that was quite funny because we said "Oh shit! They look really, really organised!"

Kay can't help but reflect on the stark contrast with her own team.

> I actually had to cut my jacket down because it was a men's jacket, and it was just hanging off me. I actually cut mine down so I could make it fit me and then re-sewed it. We were just given the men's old uniforms.

Still, Kay's time in Hong Kong was eye-opening for her. She'd use the experience as a starting point for the rest of her career, most imminently by spearheading the (ultimately unsuccessful) bid to get the 1977 Asian Women's Cup held in Australia, and more generally by expanding women's football in the country.

Sue B

Sue finally decided to take up the offer of travelling to Hong Long as part of the Australian eleven to compete in the Asian Women's Cup. Along with Connie Burns, Sue was one of only two players to represent Australia outside of the St George Budapest team.

> So anyway, I said, "Yeah, I'll go to Hong Kong." The other thing too was most of the NSW team were in Hong Kong, so that year NSW didn't win the national championships.

Sue was flattered to be asked to go to Hong Kong but found it hard to build confidence, and due to the late notice, she never had the opportunity to attend more than one or two training sessions, let alone play a game with the team prior to the Asian Cup.

> Joe only put me on for about a quarter of one game. I'm pretty sure it was against New Zealand, where we lost 3 goals to 2. I understand that the St George team had history and played together for years, and he didn't really know me as a player. My strength wasn't in ball skills, my strength was, my determination, aggression and not being afraid to go for the ball against another player.

Despite her short time on the pitch, Sue has clear memories of the conditions which confronted the team.

> I remember training, it was really hot and muggy, very different conditions to being in Sydney. On match days, it was really exciting to be sitting in the stadium with so many spectators cheering on all the teams.
> I watched the games, of course, and I think we had a good chance of winning, but it just didn't come to fruition.

Having only met Connie as part of the Ingleburn RSL side that toured New Zealand earlier that year, Sue had little knowledge of the others and little time to get to know them. She is happy to say that they welcomed her and she has fond memories of her time in Hong Kong.

> The St George team were welcoming and I had Connie and Jim for support whilst in Hong Kong. I went sight-seeing and shopping with some of the team members and I enjoyed getting to know them. Kim Coates took me on board and was really supportive and helpful. We forged a good friendship whilst in Hong Kong and I really appreciated her ability to make me feel so welcome. I also enjoyed the company of the younger players…they were always fun to hang around.

While Sue has lost touch with the members of the team, she has recently become aware of the fight for recognition the team has taken up with Football Australia and has some strong feelings about the issue.

> The way I see it is that there are two sides to it. One side is that they weren't selected following the normal processes but having said that, there weren't those processes around at that time. I mean, the selection process has changed over time anyway, but St George was the best team in Sydney by far, back then. And I believe if there was a selection process for the Australian team then many of the players would have been selected.
>
> The team was recognised as an Australian 11. They went over to Hong Kong and they played in an International tournament representing Australia—so you can't get away from that, can you?
>
> I think there should be the recognition because that team were the pioneers. They got permission to play for Australia and then went into the Asian Cup. It's history. The team should be recognised.

Kim

The welcome and the trip reside more vividly in Kim's mind than some of the others, and she has many specific memories of her time in Hong Kong—and the journey to get there!

> Oh, we had a lot of fun.

I remember the plane ride to Hong Kong, mainly because that was the very first time I'd ever been in an airplane, and I had friends give me a bit of a farewell party the night before. They've taken me to see a movie and then go out for drinks and unfortunately, the movie they took me to see was *Airport 75*. And I was going on the plane for the very first time the next day!

The excitement there was within the group of players and then when we got to the airport and got on the plane. Some of us had never been on a plane before so it was a lot of excitement! When we arrived, the welcome we got from the people involved was memorable. That was really an experience because I've never experienced things like that before.

For Kim, the fact that she was representing her country was the most important part of the whole trip. The camaraderie she felt with the other girls, the excitement of first-time plane travel, the novelty of Hong Kong—all of it was important, but none of it compared to the pride she felt from that fact.

When we got down to the stadium, it was a huge, big stadium compared to what I'd ever experienced playing in before—just walking out onto a field that was actually a decent field, no bare patches or cows or things on it!

I remember when we got to go down there for the first game, and the opening ceremony. We walked out behind the Australian flag and stood out in line with all the other countries in the middle of the field and had all these people in the stadium watching you. It was overwhelming.

It made me proud to be Australian, but also made me scared in wanting to make sure I represented Australia properly. I wanted to do my country proud, and I did not want to let any of those other girls down by not playing my role or not doing what I needed to do.

I remember one game there was an Australian naval ship that had docked in Hong Kong and we had a lot of the sailors come and watch us play. It was quite an experience to look up in the stadium to see all these sailors up there cheering for us—for Australia—and that was a really good experience.

But I had a wonderful time. I remember quite a few of us going down to this tailor to get special shirts made-up with this female soccer player on the back as a design, and our names and Australia on the front. And I remember I was very excited because we all got those made up.

The quality of the opposition surprised the Australians, but Kim remembers how high the level of play was on her own side, too.

Some of the teams we played against! I remember some of the girls, I'm not sure if it was Thailand, and the New Zealand girls were very strong and they were around about our size, you know, our build and that. But some of the Asian countries and girls were a little bit smaller, but my God, they were fast, they were really fast.

I enjoyed the games. They were all played in very good spirits.

I have some memories of the magnificent goals being scored. I remember Trixie's goal. I think that was the first goal for her in the tournament. That was a brilliant goal, as always from Trixie.

I remember in one instance we were getting very heavily attacked and I was playing defence. I can't remember against which team. And Sue was doing a great job in goals, but I was getting checked pretty heavily. And I remember going up for this header to clear out a shot on goal, and Trudy was just behind me, and I remember that I felt very proud that we cleared that because that was a really big attack.

Unknown to the team at that point, that moment would be captured and become one of the defining images of the team playing in the first Asian Women's Cup in Hong Kong.

It was quite a strange thing because when we came home, someone had taken a photo of that defensive play and we were actually on the front page of the *Daily Telegraph*. Fortunately, my mother kept a copy of that. So, I've got a copy of me on the front page of the *Daily Telegraph* with Trudy saving a goal. Although they didn't get our names right, but I don't care, it was great. I knew it was me!

It was in *The Telegraph* on the 4th of September 1975, under the heading, "Look what our girls are doing".

But not all memories are happy ones. A painful injury caused Kim to leave the field, but not by her own accord:

> I had one incident, where I'd been injured and they had to stretcher me off. And I was quite embarrassed because it took about eight or nine of them to carry me on the stretcher because they were so small!

Just as Kim's memories are strong, so are her feelings about representation. While Kim doesn't generally involve herself in the politics of the game, she has some strong opinions on Football Australia's decision not to recognise the 1975 Asian Cup tour. She firmly believes the team should be given full acknowledgement and presents a strong argument in its favour.

> I don't agree with it. We had no control over who was responsible for women's soccer in those days. We came under the banner of the Australian Women's Soccer Association. And the Football Australia chairman or president at the time recognised us as an Australian 11 and we were able to wear the green and gold. So, from my perspective, we were representing Australia.

It's a common argument that the team that travelled to Hong Kong was not a national team, as none had been selected at that time. The 1979 series against New Zealand was officially recognised as the first true 'A' international tournament attended by an official Australian team. Kim, though, believes this is a true injustice, and has several reasons to back up her claim.

> Our team wasn't just a club side because, although we had a number of St George players, you could say I was also a Blacktown Workers' player and Connie and Sue came from Ingleburn. So, it wasn't just the St George team, it wasn't a club team, it was virtually the 1974 National Championship-winning New South Wales state squad with a couple of other players.
>
> To me, once we were given permission to wear the green and gold and given permission to have the Australian XI on our shirts and all that, we were Australian. We were representing Australia as an Australian team.

The politics that went on—and is still going on now—I'm trying to stay out of. I don't feel it's right for the girls who represented, and there wasn't one person in that team that didn't represent Australia as far as I'm concerned. They were that proud to be selected to play and represent Australia in an overseas tournament.

They were the first non-club side to represent Australia in an overseas tournament and it was the first Asian Cup as well. This was the first Asian Cup, which saw representation from multiple countries. And I think in that sense, it deserves to have that recognition.

One of the biggest problems with the lack of recognition, for Kim, is that some of the players never had another chance to get their caps—meaning that they essentially had that moment stolen from them. Kim also supports the suggestion of Roman numerals to help keep caps in order.

Some of the ladies from the 1975 squad didn't go on to represent the States or Australia. They never got given the opportunity to get that 1979 cap because some of them retired and so forth, but I believe they're still entitled to be recognised.

I also think there's some issues that come up sometimes around how do you renumber the caps—like I'm cap #5, but if you take into account the 1975 team, do I still stay capped at #5? Well, it was an Australian 11 team. So, if you don't want to change the numbers, switch to Roman numerals. Cap 1 in Roman numerals, or Cap 2 in Roman numerals. So, you're not changing the existing cap numbering. You're just recognizing that they were the first Australian 11 team.

Lyn

Lyn can't recall many details of the games played at the Asian Women's Cup but does remember that she was called on in the final game of the tournament.

I honestly have gone blank on the actual games. The only thing that I remember is when I did actually get onto the pitch, I think I replaced Gundy Zarins and my whole thinking was: "Don't stuff this up!"

The crowds were amazing because we hadn't been used to that sort of thing. The atmosphere and the crowds were fantastic. But as I said, just trying to remember the actual games themselves is just a blur.

Like many of the others, one thing she does have a clear memory of is how the conditions in Hong Kong had much more of an adverse effect than any of them had expected. But more than that, the entire trip changed Lyn's life and perspectives on the world—even if she remembers things a little differently than others might.

I do remember the humidity. Going to training and you'd be basically sweating by the time you even got there, let alone doing a little bit of training. We used to train in the mornings because we played the games in the evenings because of the humidity.

I mean it was my first overseas trip, so it opened my eyes to travel and things like that. And I remember the camaraderie between the various teams and particularly between the New Zealanders and the Australians. Obviously, because we have common ground in a way.

The way that it was set up in Hong Kong was fantastic. Putting us up in a hotel and just generally looking after us.

I was reading something the other day and again I don't even remember from where, the New Zealanders said that when they won the final game, a lot of the spectators weren't happy with it. But I just I don't even remember that. Oh, I was totally oblivious, but I can tell you now most people say I'm totally oblivious to things anyway! At work I had a sign set up for me: "Queen Oblivious"!

Aunty Tarita

Even though Aunty Tarita had mixed feelings about going due to her personal life, her time in Hong Kong was extremely important to her and remains a core part of her memory.

Honestly, I enjoyed the time I was there.

The weather. I've never seen weather like that. They tell me that's how

Melbourne is. It's really hot, so we think we'll go out, then all of a sudden there's this big downpour and there's a flood and everything comes past you. It's just amazing.

I was in a hotel, very elite, very nice. Up on the 20th floor and when you looked out the window, what do you reckon was screening down there in the picture theatre – it was "Towering Inferno"! I thought that was comical.

I remember walking through the blooming markets and trying to hold my breath. But I had to breathe after a while and the things that they do! Crack the neck of the duck, cut the throat, get the blood, put it in this white powder, stir it up, make a gel. I just couldn't believe how fast they were.

I really got on well with the other team members, because I was open and respectful of their mixed cultures. Like the Malaysian team—I once paid for all of them to enjoy a flavoured milk, and one of the young ones wanted me to adopt her, she loved me so much.

Fascinating country.

An adventure with a teammate has stayed with Aunty Tarita all these years.

Christel and I were going to go out and have an adventure and there's this little fella came out. He was an Indian, he had the turban on, and he had his little lace handkerchief. He's got the handkerchief out and he saw the two of us standing there and he's trying to get us a Mercedes taxi and we both think of the money!

Anyway we said, "No mate, it's alright," so a taxi is going past—we whistled the taxi. We were real Australian bushies, although Christel is German, and we got in the taxi and as we're going along, all is well for a little while. And this fella turns around and he says, "Very sorry, my machine is broken." And that was the thing telling you how much you're going to pay. And he said it was broken.

And Christel says, "No worries, mate, pull over. I'll fix it. I'm a motor mechanic." Yeah, I'll never forget that as long as I live. He threw us out. I don't know how we got back, but we did!

It was a good experience.

Sue Larsen

Sue recalls the unique experiences of being a young girl in a foreign country for the first time. Since she was so young, she took her mum with her as an escort, which gave her a unique experience.

> When we got over there, you weren't allowed to drink the water you weren't allowed to do this, you weren't allowed to do that, so my mum came along. She was the manageress of the team and she, Trixie, and Kevin sort of took us under their wing. He, having been in the Navy, knew a lot of the good, safe restaurants and things to eat, so he would take us around to the different markets and take us around to the different restaurants and made sure that everybody was looked after and eating the right things.
>
> It was such an experience for everybody and the driving in the cabs…! You know the roads weren't wide enough for two cars, but they always managed to fit three, and things like that. When you'd go over a bridge and you'd see all the people living between the freeway in just tin sheds like in little humpies, that's something that we'd never seen or experienced, so it wasn't just soccer it was a lifetime's experience of seeing a different country. The shopping was pretty cheap as well.

But the trip was not all about the cultural and shopping experiences—there were football games to be won. Sue reflects on the lessons she learned from the wins and from the losses.

> I thought we were going to go over and win. We were undefeated here in Australia, but we came across some really good players, and to be able to play at that elite level was an experience that probably helped ground me. I was probably so cocky and had to realise that there were other players in the world that could play as well as us. You have to remember; I was only 16 years old.
>
> That really sort of stuck in my mind and when I came back. I didn't take the winning for granted anymore. There are players out there that

could beat you, and as I matured, so did my game and my attitude towards the game.

Sue went onto represent her State in a number of National Championships.

I played State from the first competition in 1974, and in eight or nine others. I don't remember the years. I think I played in most of them. I've been to all the States and Territory. And yeah, done it all.
But her time in Hong Kong was the highlight of it all.

Vickie

For Vickie, representing Australia was paramount to her experience in the Asian Women's Cup. She has lots of memories of the opulence of Hong Kong, too. She also reflects on how it was the first time she truly felt taken seriously as a footballer—not just as a "woman footballer", but as a *player of sport*.

The opening ceremony was very, very wet. That's probably the first thing that comes to mind.
I remember the fact that we got to stay in a hotel that was pretty exciting because at that stage we really hadn't done much of that sort of traveling and staying in a high-class hotel.
And the fact that we had green and gold tracksuits, and we were representing the country was really exciting. And the fact that people over there actually seemed to see women's soccer as being a serious thing.
We'd been trying to get recognition for our soccer skills, I think for quite a while and I remember, prior to that guys would come out from the newspapers and they would make us pose doing our hair or putting makeup on and that sort of stuff, like it was such a novelty for them.
And yet when we arrived in Hong Kong, it was serious. We were a bit freaked out. I was freaked out by the fact that, my goodness, maybe we were actually going to lose some of these games! It was a bit scary.
I remember worrying that the dye in my tracksuit was going to run! I know we weren't supposed to drink the water. I remember that. I remember going shopping. That was pretty exciting, and getting clothes

made that you could go in one day and get them back the next day. That was pretty impressive, and not wanting to eat most of the food because I was very conservative.

There were thousands of people watching us play. Women's soccer was unheard of, so the fact that there were lots of people there watching us was great. I had my mum and dad and my brother there as well, so it was exciting—they were excited as well.

While Vickie doesn't remember much about the games, she does recall her fondness for playing in the rain. And, of course, she has mild regrets that her Australian side didn't scrape the win—but still believes they did their best.

I don't remember much about the games, except that they were tough but competitive. I wasn't used to even having other teams score goals against us.

Not having seen much of overseas women's soccer, we really had absolutely no idea about who we were going to come up against. But to be honest, I thought that we served the country really well. I think we did a good job with the preparation that we had. We didn't have the kind of things that they have now, like physios, volunteers for everything and managers or volunteers that take home the jerseys and wash them.

I remember thinking that it would have been really nice to win, but then I was really excited when we got this bracelet that says the First Asian Cup, which was really cool.

I learned a lot at that stage about the fact that, there will always be new things to learn and there was always scope for improvement.

I loved playing in the wet, so I kind of enjoyed it when it was raining. I was renowned for my slide tackles, and I loved falling in the mud and ending up filthy. So, it was pretty cool playing in the rain!

I guess at the time we were just so focused on the whole soccer thing. Our whole lives revolved around soccer. We would spend all of that time, training, playing, talking soccer, planning a strategy, let's practice or, let's play soccer, tennis, or let's get down to the park.

It was just such a consistent thing and that continued the whole time we were over there. You know, we were pretty obsessed with the whole thing. I'm sure we did the touristy thing, but I don't remember it.

In terms of the soccer, it was an amazing experience and I was really grateful to have that opportunity. I was just so glad that we got to go. And do it with people that you knew.

Reflecting on Football Australia's decision to not recognise the tour, Vickie has her own strong thoughts on the issue.

Look, in my mind, we were probably the best players in the country that went and the fact that we were from New South Wales was irrelevant because I think they would have been hard pressed to find any other players that deserved to go more than we did.

My personal opinion is I think we should be recognised. But I'm not one for stirring the pot. So, I don't usually say very much, but I really think we represented the country, and we did it well. We played in an international tournament where people *recognised us as being the Australian team.*

We were representing the country and I think we deserve to be recognised as representing the country.

The New Zealand Experience

New Zealand were in a similar position to Australia at the point of invitation in 1975. In order to send a team to the tournament, they needed to quickly set up an interim National Association. Team members were eventually selected from the leading clubs on the North Island, with five from Wellington, three from Palmerston North and seven from Auckland. Barbara Cox, the captain of the New Zealand team, recalls how the New Zealand Women's Soccer Association (NZWSA) was formed in 1975.

The secretary of Auckland received an invitation, and I don't recall whether it was from Charles Pereira or Veronica Chiu asking for a New Zealand team to come to the tournament. And that was when we were probably ready as an association to actually form a New Zealand Women's Football Association.

So I think that just sort of hastened the whole thing. The invitation came in May 1975.

Discussions were then held with New Zealand Football and then I think it was probably in August that the tournament was held. It was probably the end of June, beginning of July that the meeting was held and there was a New Zealand Football counsellor present and so basically an interim committee was chosen and that was how New Zealand Women's Football was formed.

Wellington was the first Association to form in 1972 and then Auckland followed in 1973. And the team was chosen from just Auckland and Wellington players, and I think sometime at the end of the year, Canterbury formed their association.

Although inexperienced the New Zealand team went onto to win the inaugural Asian Women's Cup.

I think there were about three or four players that had represented New Zealand in softball, so obviously they had had international experience, but for the majority of us, we'd never, ever played in an international tournament, let alone played international football.

We had no idea what we were facing. We knew what Australia was like though because we'd been to Australia. Well, I should say Sydney. We played against Ingleburn and St. George. I think there was one other team as well, Blacktown, I think. So, we actually knew some of the Australian players better than we knew the Wellington players!

So we went to Australia, played those three teams. I think it was at the end of 1973 and then we went back again, maybe it was 1974 but we didn't play them again, I don't think. But I do remember Pat O'Connor, because I actually marked her—she was playing striker at that stage and I was playing central defender, so I was actually marking her in one of those club games.

Unlike Australia, New Zealand, upon their return as the winning team were widely celebrated and recognised as national team players—Football Ferns.

When we came home the people, the reception that we got was amazing. I mean, we had the TV there, and we had a formal press conference at the airport. Certainly, a lot of publicity.

I think that's what hastened the development of the game. Suddenly people saw that we could play as well.

While the team didn't physically receive commemorative caps as a sign of recognition, the players were included as national representatives of New Zealand Football.

> We didn't get any caps; it just went down in our records. Nothing formal, we were accepted as that.
>
> I think it was partly because we had a New Zealand counsellor involved. The late Harry Dods was present at the inaugural meeting, and he reported back to New Zealand Football. He was actually a friend of my husband who became the first president. Roy asked him to attend because we had to get approval from New Zealand Football, one to travel and one to be accepted formally as an Association.
>
> He went onto become Chairman of New Zealand Football.

Barbara recalls the competition they faced and the battle against Australia, foreshadowing the beginning of the rivalry which is still very much alive today.

> It was an amazing tournament. It was very well organised. We were in a fantastic hotel.
>
> The competition was good. We had a real fight against Australia, which we always do. It's a highly competitive contest between the two of us and you never know whether you're going to win until the final whistle blows.
>
> We didn't struggle against Hong Kong and Malaysia, but Thailand was hard. Thailand and Australia were our hardest games and I don't know whether they told you, but our understanding was that Thailand had been in camp for six months and they were all from the local Air Force, I think it was.
>
> They were very good.

New Zealand's first national championships were held in Christchurch in 1976. They amalgamated with New Zealand Football in 1999.

Maybe because of the success in Hong Kong, but by 1976 we had a national tournament in Christchurch and then obviously there was Canterbury and so there was something like six associations by the end of the following year.

And then it just slowly grew, and basically every province had a women's association. We eventually decided to join the men's Association at the AGM in November 1999.

In short, the recognition of the New Zealand women's team—while still not full recognition—was important to the development of football in the country. In the same way, the Australian 1975ers pioneered the sport. So, the question remains: where was their matching fame?

Part 4
1976 AND BEYOND
Pat and Joe

After NSW won the inaugural 1974 national championship under Pat and Joe's guidance, they followed up with victories in 1976 and 1977. In the latter year, the local metropolitan competition included Ku-ring-gai, Manly, Nepean, Eastern Suburbs, St George, Sutherland, Canterbury and South-Western districts, and had more than 200 teams.

In addition to Pat's significant input as a player and captain, Joe's coaching contribution to the development of women's football cannot be ignored. All who played under Joe regard him as one of the greatest influences on their individual successes and the growth of the women's game. Interviews with those women players mention him time and time again with the highest of praise. The echo is the same over and over again: *"I just can't believe Joe O'Connor is still not inducted into the Australian Hall of Fame."*

After the 1975 Asian Cup tour, Jim Selby replaced Joe as the National Coach in 1976 and decided to omit some of the older and more experienced members from his first Australian national team. This included Pat and her good friend Trixie Tagg. Jim and Connie Selby are lifelong friends of Pat and Joe, the couples having met while Jim was coach of the Ingleburn RSL ladies' team in the 1960s. Pat reflects on the decision with grace and positivity.

> It was obvious that people at that stage, people with the right tickets, that was the way we had to go. And you know, Joe had done his bit. He'd brought it forward as far as he could. And no, there was no animosity. Joe was quite happy that Jim had taken the trouble to do the courses and I think, if I remember right, Jim took over and then Joe was assistant for one

of them. But there was no animosity at all. We were quite thrilled that Jim had done that.

In 1977, Pat again approached the ASF in an attempt to get a women's game between Australia and New Zealand as a curtain-raiser to the men's FIFA World Cup qualifying match between the Socceroos and the New Zealand 'All Whites'. The men's match was scheduled to be played on 27 March in Sydney.

Unfortunately, this time, Pat's request fell on deaf ears. The ASF executive voted 8–2 against the proposition. Sadly, due to the unavailability of historical records no formal reason for the decision was found.

After returning home to Sydney from the National Championships in Perth in 1977, Pat and Joe decided that a change was needed.

Although both Pat and Joe attended the 1978 international championship in Taiwan it was the last time the pair would grace the international football stage. The family moved to Perth in 1978 and, while she continued to play, Pat declined to stand for re-election to the AWSA executive in 1979.

> When we were travelling to Australia by boat our first preference was to settle in Perth, but we were advised that Sydney offered more employment opportunities, so we travelled there. When Kirk turned 18, we had a decision to make. While we were at the 1977 National Championships in Perth, we had a look around. We decided then it was time to hand over the reins and move to Perth. So, we sold the house and moved over in 1978.
>
> We enjoyed 10 fabulous years and then we came over to WA. I captained WA in 1978 and we won the national championships in Newcastle. And I played for a few club sides over here.

Jim Selby took the Australian national team to the 1978 World Women's Football Invitational Tournament held in Taipei, Taiwan in October 1978. He stayed as the national coach until 1985, when he declined re-election and Fred Robins took over.

Jim has spent a lifetime in football and, in 2022, is in Tonga with his wife Connie. Connie's position is the National Women's Team Head Coach preparing the team for OFC World Cup Qualification Tournament, and Jim is the National Men's Team Head Coach/Technical Specialist Coach & Player Development and has also been Technical Adviser for the Women's National Team.

Pat played for another five years while in Western Australia and finally hung up her boots in 1983.

> I played in the state team in 1978 and then I played five years with club sides here and then decided it was time. It just broke my heart.

Pat was inducted into the FFA Hall of Fame in 2001. However, all didn't go to plan.

> I was inaugurated into the Australian Soccer Hall of Fame. And every year this happened up until they had a presentation in Sydney. I was contacted and it said I could bring a partner with me and everything will be paid for.
> And then there was some change in the system of the men's Soccer Federation, they changed over from one group of men to another.
> I don't know what happened, but then I got a letter saying that everything had changed in the men's Federation. And there were no funds to pay for people like myself—who were now in another state—to travel to Sydney for this presentation. They arranged for folks like me to have their certificates presented in their home state. So, mine was presented at a gathering in Perth.

Of course, this didn't take away from the pride of the award—or any of the hard work that went into it. Pat and Joe lived the rest of their married lives happy, and proud of what they'd done together.

In 2020, Trixie Tagg visited her old friends and found a welcome just as warm as she had all those years before. Trixie explains:

> I visited Pat and Joe O'Connor and their son Kirk and daughter-in-law Dianne with my husband Bob at the beginning of 2020. I was so happy and appreciative to see them for the first time after 40 years, but sadly our planned stay in Perth had to be cut short, because the borders were closing because of COVID.

Sadly, not long after, Joe O'Connor passed away in 2021. Pat and Joe's son, Kirk, kindly provided the following words in recognition of the contribution of his parents to the development of women's football in Australia and, in a broader sense, their gift to the sporting community and culture in Australia.

From the first day Joe and Pat O'Connor watched a social game of ladies' soccer in the park behind their house they were both won over by the opportunity for fun, fitness and community involvement.

From there Pat joined in, and Joe became the coach, and they quickly established a reputation for taking what had been a good old laugh for all involved into a far more serious and rewarding sport for all involved.

A new team was formed in the heart of the city of Sydney, which was aligned with the first division something semi-pro men's soccer club, Sydney Football Club Prague (some years later, this team moved to the St George Budapest Soccer Club).

Players were found from local Aussie girls looking for a serious sporting challenge and by advertising amongst the recently arrived migrant community.

And when I mention 'community', I have chosen this word carefully because it was primarily this forming and nurturing of the community of women footballers where Joe O'Connor stood tallest amongst his peers.

The only entry requirements to join Joe's team was that you loved fitness and football, were serious about giving it your best (no matter what your standard) and that you positively contributed to the collective whole.

Weekends saw a never-ending stream of visitors to Bass Hill in Sydney's west and the home of Joe and Pat. The door was open to everybody, and it seemed at the time that everybody came through that door (often in multiple sessions a day).

Trainers were laced and the homemade football tennis court in the big backyard got a serious workout for hours on end. It didn't matter what club you were from: if you wanted to join in, then you were always welcome.

Boyfriends, husbands, brothers, and sons were all welcome to join in, even in training, as long as they contributed positively to Joe and the girls' football community.

To have won as many games as this community of female footballers and their coach did was amazing. However, it pales into insignificance when compared against the social benefits that accrued for each and every one of those participants.

And when it was dark through the week and a ball wasn't being kicked, Joe and Pat beavered away in committees (metropolitan, state, and interstate), organising fixtures, making sure the girls each had a kit they could be proud of (as good if not better than most men's teams), and promoting the women's game to the Australian soccer hierarchy and the media.

When I say Joe was a legend I do not exaggerate. He exemplified the wonderful gift that many migrants bring to our country, and, in return, he was given the most wonderful life in Australia being part of 'his' community.

Trixie

After her return from Hong Kong, Trixie started to take up an interest in coaching. An offer from Rale Rasic (then the St George men's team coach) led her to Marconi, where she became player-coach in 1978.

Rale approached me and said, "Trixie, why don't you bring the girls across to Marconi? We can give you your own training field, we will supply the jerseys and you will become part of our club?"

I am sad to say that at this stage St George men's club was struggling financially and there weren't that many people supporting them.

I put it to the parents and the players, and they all said yes. We played with pride for Marconi for just over two years, 1978 to 1981.

All that time, from 1967 through to 1981, we were undefeated. We never lost a game.

The clubs Prague, St George and then Marconi they all received us with open arms and the spectators were so supportive. Sometimes when the men's teams played afterwards, and they were making some mistakes, some of the male spectators were yelling—"Bring the girls back on!"

Honestly, I have the fondest memories of being a player, of being a coach. Wouldn't have missed it for quids. Lasting friendships.

Trixie's love of coaching grew from that early introduction, eventually leading to the cherished appointment in 1981 as the National Head Coach of the Matildas. And a member of the only all-female coaching group to tour with a national Australian team in the history of the game to date.

> I had become interested in coaching. From 1974 until 1977, Joe O'Connor was coach of the NSW State team, and then we had Dave Wardell, Tom Petrov, and Andy Clues in 1981. Jim Selby encouraged me to join his coaching camps for girls. That was all done voluntarily. We never received any money, but we got meals and a bed and that was it. But it was just the best time.

The movement of women into leadership and decision-making roles such as coaching was a significant challenge to the male-dominated sport at that time, and not all women were treated with respect and acceptance. Many faced gender discrimination and marginalisation by male-run clubs, male administrators, and male players. Trixie found herself the only female participant at the early coaching courses, but the encouragement and support from friend and mentor Jim encouraged her to continue.

> I decided to do a second coaching course, and once again I was the only female candidate, and once again Jim Selby told me that I was in the top three. So, I think us females can mix it with the males when it comes to coaching. It doesn't matter whether you're male, female, or in between, if you have the right attributes and you're genuinely interested in putting something back into the game.
>
> I'd love to see more girls become coaches. We're not doing too bad, actually; I think we've got four female coaches now. Yeah, it's great to see. Fantastic to see.
>
> I did quite a few of those coaching camps. Once with 53 girls and Rale Rasic as Head Coach. I was then appointed assistant NSW coach. I was

assistant to Dave Wardell, Tom Petrov, Andy Clues, and Oscar Gonzales. Then in 1985 I was Manageress for John Doyle and Alan Lytton. Quite a few years later I assisted Leigh Wardell at the U-19 Nationals in Canberra, which NSW won.

I was the only female candidate.

Trixie's big break came in 1981.

I had worked with Jim as assistant coach, and in early 1981, he said he could not go to New Zealand, and the tour had already been organised. And he said, "Trixie would you be interested?" And I said, "Of course", but I didn't know whether I would be appointed.

I've got a lovely letter to say that I was appointed, and the tour ended up going to New Zealand. We played four games including a full Test, in which eight Matildas earned their first cap.

And we won all four games. In the squad were captain Cindy Heydon, Sandra Brentnall, Julie Dolan, Sue Monteath, Sharon Wass, Kerry Hetherington, Leanne Priestly and Leah Wright. So quite a few strong and skilled players.

It was just a fantastic tour and to this day in 2022 it has been the only Matildas all-female touring party. We had Irene Snead from northern NSW as tour leader, Betty Hoar from Victoria was the team Manageress, Annette McKenzie from South Australia was the physiotherapist, and I was the proud Coach.

In 1979, to mark the Matildas' first full 'A' international against New Zealand, FFA introduced commemorative caps in recognition of those who represented Australia. Julie Dolan, the captain of the team for that game, was bestowed the honour of cap number one for that game. Players have since received numbered caps according to when they wear the green and gold—naturally, a point of contention when compared to the treatment of the 1975ers.

I recently found out that eight of the players in that squad that played against New Zealand, which was the one and only official test there, received their Matildas caps. I was unaware of that at the time.

Trixie was also involved as the coach of an NSW Under-16 team tour to Los Angeles in the United States at the beginning of 1981.

> We played six games. We won five and we drew one. Julie Dolan was the captain, Kym Lembrick vice-captain and I had another vice-captain, Susie Stevenson from the South Coast—a wonderful, wonderful player.
>
> Her mom is still involved in women's football down there. She must be into her 90s. Her mom and her brother came along as tourists. So, we had two spectators cheering us on.

Family life and work finally resulted in Trixie stepping back from full time coaching in 1985. At that time, women were unable to finance themselves in the game and in particular coaching positions were rare. But stepping down didn't end Trixie's involvement in the game.

> I had two babies straight after each other and then I found out I was appointed to Concord High in 1985. I was there for more than 20 years, and I became heavily involved in football. Actually, I was there for 25 years. There was another five years previous where I introduced football to Birrong, Burwood, and Bankstown.
>
> I also had a wonderful time at Concord High. I've got lots and lots of memories and I had very supportive principals who allowed me to introduce football. I took teams to football tournaments, both indoor and outdoor. I'd come back for a week and then I'd be off again with the girls or the boys. And I was lucky to get a foot into the door with the zone soccer for the boys. Then, later on, I became a regional Coach/Manageress at different times. Furthermore, I was a Combined HS selector.

Since her retirement from school, Trixie has remained a lifetime supporter of the game, and recognises the importance of "giving back" to the game that she loves.

> When you reflect back, there is something that you can pinpoint that you learn from playing soccer. I think it's important for players and ex-players to contribute in some way. Put something back into the game that we all

love. For instance, join a committee, become a coach, assistant coach, or manageress. It is vital that we support football clubs at all levels. And I believe there is no *I* in the word team, and that camaraderie is vital for successful team spirit on and off the field.

I have been an administrator, I've been a coach, I've been a player, and I've been a referee. Only once in my 30-plus years involvement did someone say something negative about me, and that's when I refereed a match between two men's teams at Concord.

A spectator obviously disagreed with my decision and yelled out very loud, "Get back into the kitchen!"

I laughed because my wonderful husband, he does 95% of the cooking for us. I thought that was funny!

That's the only negative remark that I ever heard. I'm thinking perhaps people don't always agree with my decisions, but they've never fronted me.

Most importantly, Trixie has recently taken up the role of lead advocate in the fight for the formal recognition by FA of the 1975ers.

We've been very, very quiet.

Elia Santoro has helped us immensely. It is only during the last two and a half years that I've realised that we do have the proof and documentation that our 1975 Australian team should be officially recognised. The Asian Football Confederation has. There is even a YouTube video of the modern design of the Asian Cup trophy explaining that the 3 strands in each of the 2 handles represent the 6 countries that participated in the first Women's Asian Cup.

That includes Thailand, Malaysia, Singapore, Hong Kong, New Zealand —and Australia!

According to their Captain Barbara Cox, New Zealand recognised their 1975 squad many, many years ago. Their selection process was similar to ours, and each player was recognised for the matches they played, including the one against Australia. New Zealand were the deserved winners of the first Women's Asian Cup.

My regret is that the promised tours of Europe for the 1975 Asian All

Stars squad never eventuated. Our Australian players that received this honour were our Captain Pat O'Connor, Christel Abenthum, Julie Dolan, Connie Selby and me.

Seeing the 1972 English Women's team recently getting recognised and presented with their caps has given us hope for official recognition for our Coach Joe O'Connor, may he rest in peace, and our 1975 Australian women's team. Sadly, we have already lost two players, Sue Taylor and Lynn McKenzie.

We all should be proud of having played a part in our women's football journey. We're looking forward to the WWC2023 co-hosted by Australia and New Zealand.

Christel

Christel's family decided to move to Borth Queensland in 1978. She now lives in Kuranda where the family runs a farm and is close to her daughter and new granddaughter.

We have a family farm, and we have all tropical fruits, and I've been going to the markets for 30 years. It's only 90 acres, not much; that's a small farm compared to all the others.

We had a daughter when I was in Sydney, so we came up to North Queensland. I had my daughter Linda, and she's now 31 years old, and this year she just had her daughter—she's called Matilda.

Linda played soccer, but she decided to become a doctor, so you know you have to study. She studied, and now she's already seven years a fully qualified specialised female doctor all around the area here, which we need. And I'm happy that she's around and not going into the big cities.

And now we're bringing up this little Matilda. She's eight months old, and they're going to move in here. We have another house which we are fixing up for the girls so they can be close.

Maybe I'm going to produce another Matilda!

And while talking about family, Christel recalls how important the whole support network is to the women's game, both fellow women as well as male friends and partners.

We shouldn't forget to recognise the early-stage boyfriends or husbands. You have to also acknowledge that they're there and you can't do it all by yourself. You know you're in a partnership, you have to give and take.

You can't just always have your way, and then maybe that's why I would have gone full out for being a coach and probably the next national coach.

Though she made the choice to compromise her dream of national coaching to move with her family, this didn't prevent Christel from staying involved in football. She continued to coach local teams. Sadly, even now, she sees discrimination still circling the women's game.

Maybe if I would have been good enough, at the end, to be a national coach for the women's team, but like I'm here now and I was not in Sydney, so you have to choose. We had to make a living—my husband as well. I can't just say, forget everything else.

I played for the local team, Stratford, and then I was coaching the girls here for a long time, for 30 years in Kuranda. I coached all the little kids. You have to learn how to throw a ball in when you are five or six years old. And you still can see today—the main players don't know how to do it properly, or like heading a ball.

You need to get the right coaching at the right time, and that's what I have tried to do here.

But even here in Cairns, when I wanted to referee, they said, "Look, uh, women, they can't referee."

It's still happening. We have Mareeba in the National League, and I coached the girls' teams there and the coach said, "Women can't coach." It's still happening, this stigma. That part of it is not nice.

And yet, Christel ends her reflection on a note of hope—a hopefulness for the next generation.

I'll go back probably next year with the little ones. I like to coach. I like to give them the right start.

Julie

After leaving St George Budapest in 1983, Julie played with Marconi and had stints with several other clubs including Gymea Bay, Ballina, Sutherland, and Arncliffe Scots.

While Julie has retired from playing, she is still heavily involved in the game's ongoing development. Julie is currently working as the Football Technical Director at the International Football School on the Central Coast of NSW. She is involved as an ambassador for FIFA Women's World Cup Legacy '23 Program, which aims to play a critical role in raising awareness and advocacy for achieving gender equity in sport participation.

Julie also values the contribution of the pioneers of the game and in recognising its history, in which she very much has a place. Aside from her place in the 1975ers, Julie was part of the officially recognised first international women's competition in 1979. New Zealand agreed to compete in a three-test series in Sydney and Brisbane known as the Trans-Tasman Cup. Julie Dolan captained the team in the first game and as a result was recognised with the number one commemorative cap by FFA.

I think Football Australia have done a remarkable job in terms of getting the history somewhat organised so that now we've got a much better idea of who's who in the zoo, but there's still a fair way to go.

It's just the wheels turn a bit slowly and one thing is you have people in there now that are interested, whereas for so many years it was like, "Oh yeah, do we really have to?" Or "We don't have the resources to do that", or something that always got in the way. I think the encouraging sign is that people are really passionate about this stuff now.

Football Australia has drawn a line in the sand according to when the first game was officially recognised by FIFA, and I guess they had to draw a line in the sand somewhere. There's always going be people that were involved before that time, but for them that's where the official game started. I feel for everyone who feels that they've been hard done by, and I know Football Australia are aware of that. And I think that's really important and is a barrow that needs to be pushed.

Julie's opinion on the fight for recognition is somewhat different to several of her teammates on the 1975 team. She believes there are good reasons why the 1979 tour is still considered to be the first, though not that the 1975 Cup deserves no recognition at all—just that it might take some more time.

> You know, they had to draw a line in the sand somewhere.
> The powers-that-be have recognised the 1979 tour. I was talking to a couple of the officials there and they were asking me questions about the 1975 tour, so it's not that they don't want to recognise these people. I think their hands are tied somehow, but I don't think it will remain that way. I think there will be recognition somewhere along the line, which is thoroughly deserved.

Kay

After the 1975 tournament, Kay and her husband, Nick, attended a meeting with the organisers who wanted to hold the next Asian Cup tournament in Australia. The ALFC originally awarded the 1977 tournament to Australia, but it was eventually held in Chinese Taipei. Australia didn't return to the Asian Cup until 2006—the year Australia hosted the event. A team from Western Australia attended the 1980 tournament in India. Kay remembers that discrimination against women's football was a major reason for the loss.

> Here in Australia, we got absolutely no support from anybody. No government support, no recognition from anybody. No newspapers or anything.
> We were a little bit worried because we didn't know how we were going to organise it when you know we weren't even recognised by the men's Soccer Association. We didn't have the Australian Women's Soccer Association and the men barely recognised us and we all had to pay our own fares over on the plane.
> The whole environment for having the Asian Cup here in Sydney for us was impossible. We couldn't put everybody in a hotel, and we couldn't hire grounds and all that kind of stuff. And with no media coverage, we

probably wouldn't have got anybody in the grounds anyway.

So, they gave it to Taipei. And then even for our second team that went to Taipei, the Taiwanese actually paid for our girls to go. Embarrassing, hey? So, we got no government support or anything. It was all because the men's Association didn't recognise us, so everything was really tough.

And when we had the Australian Championships in New South Wales, those girls had to come, they all had to pay their own fares to get to Sydney. We arranged billets for them where we could, but it was a whole different environment for us.

After returning from Hong Kong, Kay continued her involvement in the game by trying to expand the number of women playing in the Eastern Suburbs competition.

I actually went to a few of the clubs and asked them if they'd be interested in trying to get a junior team together. At the time, all they wanted to say was, "Well, if the girls want to play, they can play with the boys when they're young."

Their parents would buy all the uniforms, take them to the games, and then the boys wouldn't pass the ball to the one little girl in the team. Then the little girl didn't want to go back anymore, so it took quite a few years before they got junior girl's teams.

But I am really impressed when I see how it is now.

Kay's team, the Rangers, moved to the Canterbury competition for a short while until Kay, who by this stage had three children, decided that it was time to retire.

It was a long way to go, hard to park and all that kind of stuff, so I didn't want to play there. Also, I had three children. After that, I sort of dropped out.

While Kay is no longer involved in the game directly, she is a staunch advocate for the recognition of the 1975 Asian Cup team by Football Australia.

It was just because of the way things were at the time, you know. We didn't have a women's soccer association. We didn't have any support and the men were not really interested in us, even to the point of aggravating us by saying stuff like "Women shouldn't be playing soccer".

They just gave us a hard time and it took a lot of effort from Joe and Pat to actually get them to give us any kind of recognition.

Sue B

When Sue returned from Hong Kong her life took on a different direction and soccer was no longer as important.

When I got to Hong Kong it gave me the bug to travel. I met a man in Hong Kong who was following the Asian Cup. He owned a soccer agency in England and he told me if I came to England, he'd give me a job managing soccer teams and travelling around Europe with them. It was agreed that I would travel to England the next year to begin the position. We kept in contact by mail.

That was my incentive to begin my travelling. So, I arranged with a girlfriend to travel by cruise ship to England. Unfortunately, she had other commitments and we had to defer the trip for another year. The agency couldn't wait for me so he gave the job to someone else. I ended up travelling a year and a half later. I didn't want to travel on my own, as I was only 18 and did not know anyone else in the UK.

I travelled and worked overseas for about five years. Working and living in England, touring Europe, working in Iceland for a 1½ years and hitch-hiking around US and Canada for six months. I am grateful for my experience with soccer as this gave me the incentive to see the world.

When Sue did travel back home, she tried to return to the game but things were never the same.

I come back every now and then from overseas, and I did play a couple of games, but then I sort of knew I'd lost the drive, it wasn't the interest, I felt fearless when I played the game before, and I knew that when I was backing off from the ball, I didn't have it anymore.

> When I played before, just going for the ball never worried me. I'd collide with anyone—I'd be just looking at the ball and going for it regardless of the consequences. I was happy if I came off the field with blood running down my knees. When I come back from overseas, I sort of lost the fearlessness.

After returning from her travels, Sue took up teaching and worked at a specialist sports high school for many years. This gave her the opportunity to still follow her passion in sport. She was a sports mentor in the school for highly gifted sporting students. She enjoyed this, which took her back overseas mentoring the school's student netball team in Hawaii.

Sue still follows the women's game. She is a keen supporter of the Matildas and is looking forward to attending the FIFA Women's World Cup when the Matildas play in Sydney.

> My son bought me a ticket to the World Cup for my birthday to see the Matildas play Ireland so I'm looking forward to that!

Kim

Though Kim kept playing after returning from Hong Kong, her career wouldn't last forever at that pace. After a couple of bad injuries to her legs, Kim decided to stop playing in 1983.

> My doctor suggested that it would be better for me to give up rather than suffer later on in life. So, I stopped playing at that level—Australian, State, and even at the social levels for quite a number of years, until I came back to NSW when my father got sick in 1994.

Kim's father was still heavily involved in soccer at that point in Sydney, and Kim's desire to pull the boots back on was too strong.

> Dad was involved with the Marayong club, and they used to play 7 a side games in the evening. I started playing for his club again, and then I caught up with a lot of the old friends from the NSW teams that I used to play

with, and against.

Collette Fitzpatrick was one of them, and she had a team that was playing in Auburn. St. Johns. I played for a few years there. Just played at the social weekend level. I then got involved with Collette and the girls and the NSW Masters soccer teams. I played the Masters from 1994 through to 2000 or 2002.

While Kim's return to the game in her local area where her dad was heavily involved was enjoyable, it wasn't quite the same as playing with the girls from St. George.

I dabbled a little bit again when I came back home, especially when I started to meet some of the old friends that I used to play with. Especially in my local area where my dad was still heavily involved, but it wasn't quite the same as playing in the old days, back in the 70s.

The game had grown. There's lot more women playing.

But it wasn't the same atmosphere. it didn't, to me have that same feeling. When you played with the girls from St George, it was like a family. I still got on very well with the girls and we had great fun, but it wasn't that family feeling. And I credit that to Pat, Joe, and Trixie and a couple of the other girls for making me feel that way when playing for St George.

While Kim believes that the game has come a long way, it hasn't always been easy for many of the women involved.

When you spoke about the game to people at work or from outside of that you did get pretty much the same sort of reaction: "How can you be playing a men's game?"; "You've got to be this type of person to do that!"

So yeah, you got quite a bit of that, but you just spent the time with the girls and your teammates and it didn't worry you. Well, it didn't worry me because I didn't *let* it worry me.

I would say that I do know it was hard and quite a few girls that I've played with over the years, some of them did get badly treated. Which was a shame. We weren't trying to prove that we are *better* than the men. We were just trying to play a game that we enjoyed playing.

But it's better now for women who play soccer. I wouldn't say it's fully accepted, but they've come a long way.

Lyn

After Lyn returned from Hong Kong, she continued to play with St George before taking some time away from the game.

> I only played in club games. My skills weren't at the level of the other girls. And they had more of a desire to go on, whereas I probably didn't have that that fire in me to do it. I mean, I enjoyed watching the game and things like that and playing it as a recreational thing, as opposed to really getting into the competitive side of it.
>
> I was probably fortunate that I went to Hong Kong. You know how they say sometimes you're in the right place at the right time.

Lyn travelled to Europe in 1977 and, when she returned, moved with the team to Marconi in 1978.

> I went with them to Marconi. But I was probably only there a couple of years and then I sort of got out of that altogether. I don't know what I did.

Lyn returned to the game in her 50s and finally hung up the boots at the age of 58, after playing some indoor and six-a-side soccer.

> Later on, through my now son-in-law—his sister played, and we ended up being in an all ages team when I was in my 50s. And that was with Carlingford Redbacks, and then we also played indoor soccer for a while. After that, we ended up doing some six-a-side games.
>
> But I was finding it very hard when it was an all-ages team and some of the girls were like 16 years old. I had to get someone to sub for me quite a few times!

After a lifetime dedicated to playing football, Lyn reflects on Football Australia's decision not to recognise the 1975 Asian Cup touring team.

I think the girls should be recognised because from my understanding the actual Asian Cup—the handles on it, represent the six teams that that were in the original Asian Cup.

I think, well if they can recognise that, then there should at least be some sort of formal recognition. And as I said, granted they weren't representative of the *whole* of Australia—but they said it was an Australian 11, they didn't say it was an Australian team.

I can understand that it wasn't an Australian representative side, but the calibre of some of those girls was just way up there. I mean, later on, and I could be wrong with this, but Christel Abenthum went back to Germany and she was playing with Bayern Munich.

Trixie came here when I think she was about 13. All the girls had a background in soccer, so they had the skills. I would think the skills nowadays are way in advance of what perhaps the skills that we had at the time, but you know, it was a different era.

Some people are talking about caps and things like that, but I think it's just basically about being recognised that it was the first International.

It was a strong team, so they may not have done as well even if they were able to get people from other States. And that would have been restrictive in itself, because to try and train together you wouldn't be able to get everyone together and you would have only been able to train when you got to Hong Kong. I just don't think that you would have had the cohesiveness of the team that went.

I just think there's a lot of political stuff that goes on.

From what I understand, it was originally only supposed to be club teams, and then it was changed. New Zealand set up their association and had a representative team, but it was still only a representative team from the North Island, which didn't include anyone from the South Island.

They won, and they were lauded when they came back apparently. And they've been recognised.

Lyn is still involved with the women she played with over 40 years ago, and enjoys watching the game.

Yeah, we still keep in contact. And it's funny. I mean, all those years have passed. And yet when we had the reunion in February 2020, it was like nothing had changed. It was really exciting to see everyone.

I sometimes think, oh I wouldn't mind kicking the ball around again, but whether the body would be able to stand up to it, I don't know!

We did have, it's probably over 18 months ago, there was a competition. And again, it was like a six-a-side competition just for the day. A knockout sort of thing where we had some of the men and about four or five of us from the women players that had a bit of a game which was nice, and that was out at Peakhurst, I think.

I still enjoy watching the game.

Aunty Tarita

Upon her return to Australia from Hong Kong, Aunty Tarita decided that her time in soccer was over. She needed to concentrate on supporting her young family.

When I got back to Australia, I packed all those things up and never watched a football game of any sort again. I felt so horrible that I couldn't walk on water for my coach. Because that man was the only person that ever gave me a sense of worth. We should have been wearing the crown. We were good because we put the work into it, and we were very good players.

If it wasn't for Aunty Tarita's sister noticing an article in the *Courier Mail*, she wouldn't have had the opportunity to tell her story and claim her role in the history of women's soccer in Australia.

I wasn't going to come into this, but my sister had the *Courier Mail*. And she said, "Are these people your team?" And I said, "Yes, they are." And she said, "Oh, it's in the paper, are you going to contact them?" And I said, "No, no, no, that's in the past. I don't want anything to do with it now." My sister is very strong-willed, and I have to obey my sister, she's older than me and she said, "You will," and so I did.

While Aunty Tarita is not interested in getting into an argument about the formal recognition of the 1975 Asian Cup touring team, she believes that they were the first women's international touring team to represent Australia and should be recognised as such.

> The point is we were the first. We were first, grin and bear it. It's as simple as that. You cannot take away from those that were the first. We were there in 1975. I believe there was some challenge, I don't get into their troubles. I don't really care one way or the other, but the truth must be heard, and the truth must be obeyed. We were there in 1975 and we did wear the green and gold.
>
> I look at it in a simple way. I don't argue with people.

Aunty Tarita now lives in Bundaberg in Queensland and hopes that her time in soccer and being the first Aboriginal woman to represent Australia at the Asian Women's Cup in 1975 will encourage other young indigenous girls to become involved in the game.

Sue Larsen

After returning from Hong Kong, Sue played with the club at Marconi until 1981 and then decided to play locally with Gladesville, before finally giving up the game in 1984.

> I played with Gladesville I think for two years because I was in that local area. But that was just at club level, and I'd come across some of the girls that I used to play with and play against all those years ago, but it was just to finish off and have a bit of fun.
>
> It was just great to not have to train three and four nights a week and then train for State on Saturdays and play Sundays and train Friday nights.

After finishing her playing career, Sue decided to give back to the game and became involved in coaching. However, at this point, while women were slowly being accepted as players, that didn't always extend to the coaching ranks. Coaching was predominately occupied by men in the 1980s even when the players were women. The movement of women into leadership and decision-making roles such as coaching was looked upon as a serious challenge to the male dominance of the sport. As such women were often subjected to levels of intimidation, accusations of inadequacy, abuse and gender-based discrimination.

> After I finished playing, I coached an under 16 New South Wales team. One year we went to Darwin and, honestly, the politics! I was so disappointed with the politics that went on and some of the backstabbing and the nastiness, that I was so disappointed with the game itself. I didn't like what it was turning into. As the game was growing, so were some of the egos. To me, there were too many trying to be chiefs.
> The game had given me so many wonderful years, so many memories. I wanted to give something back and that's why I thought I'd have a go at coaching. I had my coaching certificate because I was a PE teacher. It was just so disappointing to think that people didn't want you to give back—"You've had your turn" sort of thing. "We're going in a new direction, we don't need you."
> And that was the kind of feeling that I got. When I was coaching and I thought, well, if that's the way it's going to be, I'd rather leave with good memories rather than bad memories. I stepped away, probably too early as I still had a lot to give.

Sue moved to Queensland in 1989.

> My mum and dad had moved up a couple of years earlier and I had always come up for holidays.
> Always just my mum and dad—they were my absolute rocks, and they were my soul mates. Dad was my best friend and I miss him terribly. I had so much fun when I came up on holidays.
> But in the end, I decided, because things were not going well for me in Sydney, it was just time to step away and move to a new more peaceful lifestyle, which I absolutely love and there is no way that I would go back to Sydney. It is just so much of a nicer lifestyle up here.
> I still do my bike riding, but unfortunately with a knee replacement

I can't play soccer or anything anymore. I am mad keen on camping and have a caravan in which I travel around a bit, although COVID has delayed a bit of that.

There are many great memories, too many to recall, especially as I get older!

It was wonderful to be part of it in those days, and I would like to be recognised for the efforts and the input that we all had. I don't have the passion like Trixie still does, I mean she lives, eats and breathes soccer.

Still, though, Sue reflects fondly on her time in football—a time she hopes more and more young women get to experience without issues as the world goes on. A world she helped to pioneer.

Vickie

Vickie stopped playing club and State soccer in 1983 at the grand old age of 27.

I went overseas after I finished University, so in about 1980. I came back in 1981 and played again. I was in the State team in that year and kept playing until I moved house because I got married. I probably stopped playing in about 1983. Then I just started playing in the local club team. After I moved to the beaches I played for a local team in Manly Vale. But by that stage I was old!

One of Vickie's fondest memories of that period in her life is the role that the Australian representative jacket she wore in Hong Kong played in meeting her husband-to-be, and a long and happy marriage.

My husband decided to ask me out because I was wearing an Australian jacket to university. I remember that!

We happened to be in the same class at university, and occasionally I would wear an Australian jacket to university. I think it was interesting and different, so he chatted to me, and we ended up getting married. Have been now for over 40 years.

I was studying social work and my husband electrical engineering at the University of NSW, and we did a class together on music and human behaviour.

So, I think it was the jacket that kind of intrigued him a bit. I was excited. Yeah, it was a cool time!

Even in small ways, football has woven its way through Vickie's life, where it'll stay, in one form or another, forever.

Lynn McKenzie

Lynn was another member of the 1975 team who played alongside the women mentioned here. Sadly, she is no longer with us, after passing in 2003 following a battle with cancer. Her husband, Eric, kindly contributed a short piece detailing her career and the effect that the 1975ers and women's football had on her entire life.

Lynn was born in Birkenhead (Liverpool) in the United Kingdom and migrated to Australia with her husband Eric in 1971. Eric found work at Jordan Chemicals, and it was there that he met Pat O'Connor. Pat would often talk about her time playing soccer and this intrigued Lynn, who thought she'd give it a go, never having played competitively before.

She trained with the mighty St George Budapest team with Eric's help, and both became close friends of Pat and Joe. Having grown up with four brothers Lynn seemed to have a natural feel for the game and picked up the finer points quickly.

Through the early years, Lynn ended up playing as goalkeeper and went on to share this position with Sue Taylor. The whole team constantly worked fundraising with the target of going to the tournament in Hong Kong, and Lynn travelled with the team as a reserve to the inaugural Asian Women's Cup in Hong Kong in 1975.

Back home and as the St George team became bigger and bigger, numbers were large enough to initiate a St. George "seconds" team. Lynn and Eric took charge of the team, and they played in the same league as the main teams, with Lynn moving to centre-field to help direct the traffic.

When Eric moved to Albury as a result of work commitments, he joined the Albury Hotspurs, with Lynn often training with the team. Lynn then encouraged them to form a ladies' team and a small league ensued with the other local clubs also forming sides. The St. George "seconds" even came down to Albury for an exhibition game.

Lynn and Eric's son Duncan was born in 1977, and during this time she was invited to the very Italian town of Griffith to show a promotional video of the successful St George team. Following that visit, four local Griffith ladies' teams were formed.

In 1979, the family moved back to Sydney and settled in Quakers Hill. Lynn started playing again, but only at a very social level. She started with Polonia and was integral in forming the Quakers Hill Ladies team. She again played in midfield and often captained the side.

However, life as a full-time mum led Lynn to finally hang up the boots. Nevertheless, like her teammates, football played a huge role in her life and in that of her family. Regardless of current political recognition, she was one of the First Matildas, and her legacy lives on.

Part 5
FACTS, THE FIGHT, AND THE FUTURE
The Trophy

Teams play for victory, and the physical embodiment of that victory is the trophy. The story of the trophy for the Asian Women's Cup deserves its own section.

The trophy awarded to the winners of the Asian Women's Cup tournament has changed often since its inauguration in 1975. The chief organisers of the tournament in Hong Kong donated the first trophy, which was presented to the winners of the tournament from 1975 through to 1981. Since then, the trophy has been through several redesigns to reflect the changes and development of women's football and the growth in importance of the tournament.

In the lead up to the 2022 Asian Women's Cup, the AFC again required the trophy to have a new look. Trophy makers Thomas Lyte worked with the AFC to develop a trophy which looked at the history of the tournament and to come up with the new design that was modern but used real craftsmanship to reflect that history. It needed to honour the legacy of past champions.

The final design of the trophy for the 2022 Asian Cup included both traditional parts as well as modern features. The six handles, which were cast from six solid silver bars, point to the six participants that played in the first Asian Cup tournament in 1975. The base of the trophy promotes eight modern women footballers capturing the strength and agility of Asian women's football.

The recent redesign of the Asian Women's Cup trophy is important because it highlights the AFC's acknowledgement of the history of the tournament in Asian women's football. It also recognises the Australian team as one of the six competing nations at the inaugural tournament in Hong Kong in 1975.

The Road to Recognition

After the women had long retired from football, and many had moved to different parts of the country, they kept in contact and tried to catch up as often as they could—an occasional meal or coffee, and at Matildas' games. However, it would take 45 years before the women were to come together again as a team to fight for recognition as true pioneers of the game, and to be officially recognised as Matildas.

Elia Santoro

Elia Santoro is a strong advocate for the development of women's football in Australia. She is a Director of Special Projects Football—Event Agency and was a founding member and ex-Executive committee member for Women in Football Australia, with a vision to *encourage and to help enable girls and women to contribute effectively at the level they wish to do so in the sport.*

In 2019, Elia was busy organising the inaugural Heartbeat of Football NSL Reunion fundraising event that was to be held at the end of June at the Canterbury-Hurlstone Park RSL club in western Sydney. In the lead up to the event she received a request from Trixie Tagg, Cindy Heydon and Lyn Everett-Miller, members of the 1975 Asian Cup team, to attend. And it was from this meeting that the seeds of recognition for the 1975 Australian Women's Cup team were planted.

> I met Trixie at the event. Trixie attended with former teammates Cindy Heydon and Lyn Everett-Miller, and we had a chat and talked about ourselves and got to know each other. It was here that I first heard about the 1975 Asian Cup and the Australian team that toured. After that we kept in contact, and Trixie invited me to a couple of meetings at her home to discuss the history. Then the reunion of the team was held in 2020.

Team members Cindy Heydon, Kim Coates, Sue Larsen, Lyn Everett-Miller, Trudy Fischer, Gundy Zarins, Vickie Kohen, Connie Byrnes, and Julie Dolan all attended the reunion. Football NSW (FNSW) provided some financial assistance to offset expenses and the St. George FA donated the use of the Rockdale Ilinden Sports Centre as a venue for the occasion.

The MC for the event was Stephanie Brantz (prominent Australian sports presenter) with Rale Rasic (Former Socceroos coach and women's football supporter) as the special guest. All present enjoyed a video link up with Pat and Joe O'Connor from Perth who were unable to travel to the event.

Elia met the team members at the reunion and discussed the history of the tour and the decision of FFA years earlier to recognise international players with commemorative caps.

Most of the women were unaware of Football Australia's introduction of the commemorative cap to recognise those that represented Australia at an international tournament, and that the first had been dedicated to those in the 1979 international 'A' squad that competed against New Zealand.

After listening to the history and how they toured as an Australian team, sanctioned by the ASF, I was dumbfounded and couldn't believe that the team had not been recognised. I thought the whole process was wrong. So I decided to help them take the fight to FA and to try and help the women get the recognition they deserve.

After the reunion, Elia and Trixie gathered the research they and others had painstakingly put together and organised a meeting with FFA representatives James Johnson and Sarah Walsh on 28 October 2020 at the Sydney FA headquarters.

Elia and Trixie presented them both with a folder containing all of the research that they had compiled including newspaper clippings, video clips, and the 1975 program, as well as Trixie's green and gold jersey with the embroidered coat of arms and her Asian All Stars medal.

The FFA told Trixie and Elia that they would review the information and get back to them as soon as they could. When no response was received by 24 November, Trixie emailed FFA and included additional information, which, she hoped, would support their cause—the redesign of the Asian Women's Cup trophy for 2022.

FFA advised again that they were still investigating the available information. No comments were received from FFA in relation to the new information.

In early 2021, Trixie and Elia again contacted FFA concerned about the lack of a reply to their requests. FFA advised that due to the lack of available information, they were waiting for the completion of a research project that was currently underway in relation to the *History of the AFC Women's Asian Cup*.

This book project was initiated by the International Centre for Sport Studies (CIES) in partnership with the AFC and the FIFA Museum. The book, researched by authors and designers Kevin Tallec Marston, Francesco Marini, Fernando Roitman, and Miguel Girado, was published in January 2022.

A Decision

Football Australia finally released a press statement in May 2022:

> Following extensive research undertaken by Football Australia's historians and the recent release of the first-ever AFC Women's Asian Cup History Book, the Football Australia Board has endorsed the recommendation to celebrate the legacy and contributions of the identified players from the period of 1975 to 2013.
>
> This formal recognition will see former women's players who participated in the 1975 AFC-sanctioned tournament and players who were selected by the national governing body at the time but did not participate in 'A' internationals welcomed into the national team family.

Football Australia CEO James Johnson professed delight to see the national team family expanded to embrace players who helped lay the foundations of the game today. He said:

> It is important that we celebrate the achievements of those who have contributed so much to our game. With the FIFA Women's World Cup Australia and New Zealand 2023 fast approaching, we have a unique opportunity to spotlight women's football in Australia and the impact

these players have made.

The women who have been recognised today for their accomplishments are a shining example of the rich history of football in our country, which is so closely linked to the Australian story. We are proud to welcome them into the national team's family.

The news received widespread support and ignited a groundswell of complimentary comments in the press and on social media. Congratulations flooded the media with headlines such as provided in an opinion piece about Pat O'Connor, written by Janakan Seemampillai in *The Roar:* 'The 80-year-old who just became a Matilda.'

The players were over the moon and as Trixie Tagg commented, *"just a little bit excited!"*

An Important Distinction

However, the celebrations were short-lived when team members received a follow-up letter, which stated, in part, that the recognition would include:

> ...Addition in Football Australia's official records, presentation of a non-numbered national team cap and addition to the Matildas Alumni club.

It dawned on the team that they were not to be acknowledged as genuine Matildas nor assigned official playing numbers. A majority of the 1975 players then held a meeting with Football Australia and indicated that they would not accept the offer made by the Association. The players present stated that they would prefer to continue their claims to be recognised as true Matildas players, just as the women from the other five nations who took part in the tournament have been recognised by their respective football associations.

This was followed by much online debate, especially following a two-page article by Selina Steele in the *Daily Telegraph,* which resulted in FA's Peter Filopoulos sharing the full response on social media—stating that the team did not fit "the criteria" that was quoted above. What these criteria were was not recorded nor clarified.

This statement has raised a number of concerns from all associated with the claim for recognition. The lack of clarity in Football Australia's statement only allows for speculation as to why the decision was made.

Points of Contention

The major point of concern seems to be in relation to the perceived international status of the team that represented Australia at the 1975 Asian Women's Cup. Based on recent FIFA Statutes Article (55), *"international competitions representing national associations must be approved by the Executive Committee of the Federation"*. Writer Bonita Mersiades makes the point that it is reasonable to assume the 1975 version was similar, in which case the argument is flawed.

Based on the oral and documented evidence provided by the women players in this book, there is no doubt that the Australian Soccer Federation headed by the late Sir Arthur George AO approved the 1975 team's participation in what was, for all intents and purposes, the first Women's Asian Cup tournament.

Another point of contention relates to the lack of a formal selection process. The argument is that if "there was not a competitive process to select the team", it was not a real Australian team.

The historical context shown in this book refutes that argument. In 1975, the AWSA was only in its infancy, and was only involved with the State and National championships, which had also only begun a year earlier in 1974. The AWSA was not recognised by FIFA—but the Australian Soccer Federation were. The ASF sanctioned the tour at a meeting of the Executive in early 1975.

A further sticking point is that the majority of players selected in the 1975 squad were from one club in Sydney, St George Budapest. While this is the case, the team clearly included the best players in the country and had just successfully completed the 1974 National Championships as easy winners. If this is considered to be a decision defining point, then the history panel should look at the very similar selection process associated with the "original Socceroos" in 1922.

Nick Guoth's and Trevor Thompson's book *Burning Ambition – the Centenary of Australia-New Zealand Football Ashes* shows that the 16 Australian players who toured New Zealand was made up of eight Queenslanders and eight players from NSW. A true national team was not selected, and the best players weren't necessarily chosen.

[...] The selection process was not based on identifying the top players, but on which state federation could afford to send players to New Zealand, and who their top players were at the time. [...]it was well into the second half of the 20th century before national team selection became based predominantly on merit.

This is similar to that of the 1975 Australian women's team, but the men's team is still celebrated as the first Australian national team.

Stefan Kamasz

Stefan is a former FA board member who strongly believes in recognition of the 1975ers. He states that FA has wrongly reversed a valid decision taken by the ASF Board of Directors in 1975.

> Both should be recognised equally because pioneering international teams are chosen based on the circumstances that existed at the time, prior to what we now regard as the norm.

Unsanctioned?

References have also been made to the AFC Asian Women's Cup in 1975 not being sanctioned by FIFA. The event was organised by the Asian Ladies' Football Confederation (ALFC), a body that operated separately from the men's governing bodies AFC and FIFA.

However, this book has explained the role of the ALFC and its relationship with the AFC. Both Confederations worked together to promote the development of women's football and the inaugural Asian Women's Cup. The 1975 Asian Women's Cup has since been sanctioned as an official international women's tournament by both the AFC and FIFA.

A further point in question is that the record books show the games at the 1975 AFC Asian Women's Cup were only 60 minutes in length, when FIFA regulations generally require games to be 90 minutes. Historically the 60-minute game time regulation was in accordance with the English

FA rules for women at that time, prior to FIFA becoming involved with the women's game.

Seeking Clarity

A transparent explanation of the process and decision taken by the FA Historical Committee and Board has yet to be provided.

Newspaper references that state that all competing nations at the tournament were formally recognised cannot be verified. Apart from New Zealand, which lists its representative players starting with those that competed in the 1975 tournament, there is little information available that can confirm these statements. It is enough to accept that the countries involved sent national teams to the tournament and as such are recognised as the first women to play for each country at an international event.

While FIFA recognises certain international games as ones where a player can be considered as 'capped', not all nations use this as a way of acknowledging individual players. The awarding of commemorative caps from a historical and cultural perspective seems to be limited to countries such as Australia and Great Britain; most countries do not use this system. Research has not identified, for example, how players from the Asian nations competing in 1975 were individually recognised, if at all, and no lists of players from those competing countries can be found with associated numbers or caps. In fact, there is little reference at all in relation to the history of women's football in those Asian countries that competed at the 1975 tournament.

Meanwhile, the fight for full recognition as Matildas continues for those who represented the country in 1975.

REFERENCES

ABC News. (2021, March 26). Sex, power and anger: A history of feminist protests in Australia. *ABC News.* https://www.abc.net.au/news/2021-03-27/sex-power-and-anger-a-history-of-feminist-protests-in-australia/100030592

Apple Podcasts. (2022, November 3). On Her Mind - Recognising the first "Matildas." *Apple Podcasts.* https://podcasts.apple.com/au/podcast/on-her-game-with-sam-squiers/id1501469118?i=1000584989324

Asian Football Confederation. (2022). *History of the AFC Women's Asian Cup* [PDF]. https://assets.the-afc.com/AFC_Womens_Asian_Cup_2022/Downloads/AFC-Women's-Asian-Cup-History-Book.pdf

Brooklyn, B. (2012). The 1920s: *A Good Decade for Women in Politics* [Thesis]. University of Western Sydney.

Downes, G. (2021). *Dedicated Lives: Stories of Pioneers of Women's Football in Australia.* Fair Play Publishing

Filopoulous, P., [@peterfilopoulous]. (2022). *For everyone's awareness this was our full quote provided to the @newscorp article.* Twitter. https://twitter.com/peterfilopoulos/status/1550728520434782208?s=20&t=PswUn8j2lwqYe-UNrds7Qg

Football Australia recognises achievements of former Australian Women's Representative Players. (2022, May 9). Football Australia. https://www.footballaustralia.com.au/news/football-australia-recognises-achievements-former-australian-womens-representative-players

Freedman, S. (2023). *"Get Your Tits Out for the Lads": True Stories from a Woman in Football.* Fair Play Publishing

Guoth, N. & Thompson, T. (2022). *Burning Ambition: The Centenary of Australia New Zealand Football Ashes.*

"It meant so much to us" - Dolan remembers history-making first international. (2019, October 6). Matildas. https://www.matildas.com.au/news/it-meant-so-much-us-dolan-remembers-history-making-first-international

Krayem, V. (2021). *100 Years of Football at Wynnum*. Fair Play Publishing

Meet Australia's first female footballers caught up in a battle for recognition. (2022, February 26). *The Daily Telegraph*. https://www.dailytelegraph.com.au/sport/football/soccer-2022-meet-australias-first-female-footballers-caught-up-in-a-battle-for-recognition/news-storya/3ff7f9ebe866e772520321260af7617

Nicholls, P. (2018, September 12). *Mothering the Matildas: The trailblazers who kickstarted Australian women's football*. The Roar. https://www.theroar.com.au/soccer/longform/mothering-the-matildas-the-trailblazers-who-kickstarted-australian-womens-football-660328/

Seemampillai, J. (2022, May 12). The 80-year-old who has just become a Matilda. *The Roar*. https://www.theroar.com.au/2022/05/12/feature-proud-pat-thrilled-to-finally-be-a-matilda/

Steele, S. (n.d.). First But Forgotten: The First Matildas. *Daily Telegraph*. https://www.dailytelegraph.com.au/sport/football/soccer-2022-meet-australias-first-female-footballers-caught-up-in-a-battle-for-recognition/news-story/a3ff7f9ebe866e772520321260af7617

Stell, M., & Reid, H. (2020). *Women in Boots: Football and Feminism in the 1970s*. Australian Scholarly Publishing.

street footie LLC. (2022, December 1). *Definition of National Team - Soccer Dictionary · street footie*. Street Footie. https://streetfootie.net/glossary/national-team/

Syson, I. (n.d.). *People*. https://geordieminers.blogspot.com/p/people.html

Syson, I. (2021, April 10). *100 Years Ago Today, 8 April 1921*. https://neososmos.blogspot.com/2021/04/100-yuears-ago-today-8-april-1921.html

Watson, E. (1994). *Australian Women's Soccer: The First 20 Years*.

When it comes to the 1975ers, the cap fits | Bonita Mersiades. (n.d.). https://www.bonitamersiades.com.au/features/when-it-comes-to-the-1975ers-the-cap-fits

Williams, J. (2022). *The History of Women's Football*. Pen and Sword History.

ACKNOWLEDGEMENTS

After completing my first book, *Dedicated Lives: Stories of Pioneers of Women's Football in Australia* in 2021, I had no intention of writing another. I even promised my wife that I would take a break from women's football! And then I met Trixie Tagg, and I learnt about the plight of the 1975 Australian eleven who travelled to Hong Kong in 1975 to represent their country at the inaugural Asian Women's Cup.

I owe my involvement in the stories of those women who have become known as the 1975ers to both Trixie Tagg and Pat O'Connor, who spent many hours with me over the past year or two. Thank you for sharing your stories with me and introducing me to the other women who made up the 1975ers and kindly gave of their time and shared their stories – it was a pleasure to meet you all.

To my wife Gayle, thanks for listening again to my constant references to women's football. This time a break is definitely needed! To my family and friends who have remained interested and have supported me throughout the process - thanks.

To my friends in football, Ian Syson, Lee McGowan, Ted Simmons, Jean Williams, Trixie Tagg, Pat O'Connor, Greg Werner and Paul Nicholls. Thank you for the advice and help along the way.

A special thank you again to Bonita Mersiades of Fair Play Publishing for encouraging me to continue sharing the stories of women's football.

While this is a book about women's football, I nonetheless dedicate this book to Joe O'Connor in recognition of all he achieved in the development of women's football in Australia and for the many he influenced along the way.

ABOUT THE AUTHOR

Dr Greg Downes completed his Ph.D. in 2016 with Victoria University, in Melbourne, Australia, and currently writes, teaches, and researches women's sports history, sport management, and human services from his home in Lennox Head on the north coast of NSW, Australia.

He became interested in women's football due to the involvement of his youngest daughter Caitlin. Greg was involved in many roles over the years his daughter played club, school, and regional representative soccer in northern NSW with the Byron Bay club, including as Chairman of the North Coast Academy of Sport. He has been both clubs- and representative-team manager, club treasurer, regional-committee member, supporter, and general dogsbody.

As a parent, Greg became aware of the many injustices and discriminations faced by young girls and women in their pursuit to play the game. During this time he became involved in the fight to make his daughter's involvement in soccer an inclusive one.

While studying for his Masters, Greg used examples of these injustices faced by women involved in football as topics for his research. He came to realise that little or no research had been done on the history of women's football in Australia. The voices of the women were unheard and were yet to be written into the history of the game.

Greg's Ph.D. research topic, *An oral history of women's football in Australia*, formed the basis of his book *Dedicated Lives – Stories of Pioneers in women's football in Australia* published by Fair Play Publishing in 2019.

The First Matildas is his second book.

More really good football books from Fair Play Publishing

Hear Us Roar
Compiled by Bonita Mersiades

Encyclopedia of Matildas
World Cup Edition
by Andrew Howe and Greg Werner

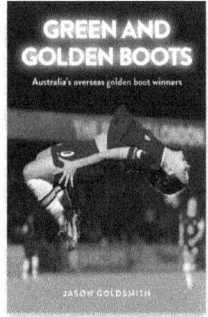

Green and Golden Boots
by Jason Goldsmith

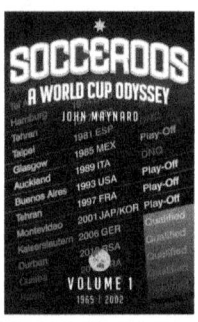

Socceroos
A World Cup Odyssey
Volumes 1 & 2
by John Maynard

"Get Your Tits Out
For The Lads"
by Sally Freedman

Football Fans In
Their Own Write
Compiled by David Picken

FAIRPLAY
PUBLISHING

www.ingramcontent.com/pod-product-compliance
Lightning Source LLC
Chambersburg PA
CBHW072056110526
44590CB00018B/3203